A COPYRIGHT PRIMER

COPYRIGHT   INFORMATION   BULLETIN   SERIES

1. Jerome K. Miller, *Using Copyrighted Videocassettes in Class-rooms and Libraries*, 1984 (out of print).

2. Charles W. Vlcek, *Copyright Policy Development: A Resource Book for Educators*, 1987.

3. Jerome K. Miller, *Using Copyrighted Videocassettes in Class-rooms, Libraries, and Training Centers*, 1987.

4. Esther R. Sinofsky, *A Copyright Primer for Educational and Industrial Media Producers*, 1988.

5. Jerome K. Miller (Ed.), *Video Permissions Procedures*, (scheduled for 1988).

A COPYRIGHT PRIMER

FOR

EDUCATIONAL AND INDUSTRIAL

MEDIA PRODUCERS

BY

DR. ESTHER R. SINOFSKY

COPYRIGHT INFORMATION SERVICES

Published and distributed by

COPYRIGHT INFORMATION SERVICES
POST OFFICE BOX 1460
FRIDAY HARBOR, WA 98250

****
Library of Congress Cataloging-in-Publication

Sinofsky, Esther Rita.
    A copyright primer for educational and industrial media
producers.

    (Copyright information bulletin; no. 4)
    Bibliography: p.
    Includes index.
    1. Copyright–United States. I. Title. II. Series.

KF2994.S56   1987   346.7304'82   87-15423
ISBN 0-914143-12-3   347.306482

DEDICATION

To my parents, Boris and Faye,

for being there–always.

DISCLAIMER

The opinions contained herein reflect the author's informed opinion but do NOT constitute legal advice.

TABLE OF CONTENTS

PREFACE

My friend's husband called with a potential copyright question. He was preparing a slide show for his firm and wanted to include a slide showing a famous actress who had died about twenty years ago. Could he use the picture? At that time, I wasn't sure and suggested he ask the firm's legal counsel since the picture might be copyrighted. Shortly afterwards, Jerome K. Miller suggested I write a book for Copyright Information Services dealing with copyright for producers of educational materials.

Considering his suggestion, I figured this should be a fairly straightforward subject to research. After all, it couldn't be as bad as fair use, that perennial quagmire. So much for wishful thinking! Pitfalls galore await the uninitiated in this area. And, we're dealing here not just with copyright (that would have been too easy!), but with other legal areas such as privacy and the Lanham Act (trademarks). To help matters, privacy, for example, is found at the state level; there is no uniform federal law. This translates into variations between court jurisdictions and, ultimately, how you may be affected.

I found many books for producers covering the finance, distribution, technical, and other aspects of film and video production. But I found little information directed to the educational producer on copyright, unless you count three- and four-volume legal treatises (written by and for lawyers) and various legal articles and cases indexed under every topic except the one you want. (Of course, the topic you do want never exists in the indices!)

Faced with the fruits of my research, I realized I couldn't cover every possible problem area. Even lawyers who frequently negotiate production-related contracts say no book can answer all the questions. [1] In addition, the copyright situation is unique to a given production's circumstances. No "standard" forms or contracts exist; everything depends on negotiations. In fact, those sources offering illustrative production-related forms usually do so with the proviso that the user alter them to fit the situation. Hence the decision to limit this work to a **primer**, i.e., a small introductory book on a subject. After some adjustments, the intended audience now includes educators, industrial trainers, and other amateur and small producers, including producers of programs for local-access cable TV channels.

The book is divided into two parts: Part I discusses key sections of the current Copyright Act; Part II focuses on specific production-related issues. By the time you finish reading this primer, you should have at least a glimmer of some of the key copyright issues you can encounter during a production. I suggest you then sit down with your lawyer to discuss how these issues affect your production situation.

REFERENCES

1. See, for example, Paul A. Baumgarten and Donald C. Farber, *Producing, Financing and Distributing Film* (New York: Drama Book Specialists, 1973), p. xxi.

SINOFSKY'S RULES OF THUMB

The following points are offered as a summary of the issues discussed in this book:

1. "Material copyrighted in one medium may be infringed by material produced in another medium." [1]

2. Educational use is NOT synonymous with fair use.

3. Non-profit, educational entities may have difficulty claiming fair use.

4. Commercial, for-profit entities will have more difficulty claiming fair use.

5. License and contract clauses are negotiable.

6. When in doubt, consult a copyright-knowledgeable lawyer.

7. It is cheaper to buy a license than settle out of court.

8. Users of copyrighted materials have some rights, but DON'T abuse them!

9. The only certain things in life are death, taxes, and claims of copyright infringement. (Apologies to B.F.)

REFERENCES

1. *Filmvideo Releasing Corporation v. Hastings*, 193 U.S.P.Q. 305, 307 (S.D.N.Y. 1976).

PART I

WHAT THE LAW SAYS

CHAPTER   1:

WORKING   DEFINITIONS

In *Through the Looking Glass*, Humpty Dumpty sneers at Alice: "When *I* use a word, it means just what I choose it to mean —neither more nor less." [1]   Humpty Dumpty was lucky he never dealt with copyright law.   His penchant for self-imposed definitions would probably land him in the midst of a copyright infringement suit.

Nuances are important in understanding and applying copyright law.   For example, **sound recordings** and **phonorecords** are not synonymous.   Therefore, though a glossary normally appears towards the end of a book, furnishing a basic list of definitions before plunging into the Copyright Act and its effect on specific production topics makes sense.   A selection of legal terms is also included since, despite my best efforts to write in plain English, "legalese" could not be avoided entirely.   Hopefully then, this chapter will prevent a widespread outbreak of Humpty-Dumpty-itis and provide a common starting point for discussing the law. [2]

ACTION.   A legal proceeding to enforce one's rights.

AFFIRM.   A higher court declares a lower court's judgment is valid and correct.

APPEAL. The losing party applies to a higher court to rectify the lower court's decision.

AUDIOVISUAL WORKS. "Works that consist of a series of related images which are intrinsically intended to be shown by the use of machines or devices such as projectors, viewers, or electronic equipment, together with accompanying sounds, if any, regardless of the nature of the material objects, such as films or tapes, in which the works are embodied" (compare with **motion picture**). [3]

CERTIORARI. Based on a petition to an appellate court, an order, when granted, for a lower court to send its record of a particular case up to the appellate court. The appellate court may grant or deny certiorari (i.e., agree or refuse to review the case) as it sees fit, without stating its reasons.

COLLECTIVE WORK. "A work, such as a periodical issue, anthology, or encyclopedia, in which a number of contributions, constituting separate and independent works in themselves, are assembled into a collective whole." [4]

COMMON LAW. Law developed through court decisions as opposed to statutes and regulations.

COMPILATION. "A work formed by the collection and assembling of preexisting materials or of data that are selected, coordinated, or arranged in such a way that the resulting work as a whole constitutes an original work of authorship." [5] It includes collective works.

COMPLAINT. In civil cases, the first formal step in instituting a law suit. The document is filed with the federal courts.

CONSTRUCTIVE KNOWLEDGE. Ignorance of the law is not an excuse; that is, you can be held responsible for copyright infringement.

COPIES. "Material objects, other than phonorecords, in which a work is fixed by any method now known or later developed, and from which the work can be perceived, reproduced, or otherwise communicated, either directly or with the aid of a machine or device. The term 'copies' includes the material object, other than a phonorecord, in which the work is first fixed." [6]

COPYRIGHT ACT. The General Revision of Copyright Law which passed Congress in 1976 and took effect on January 1, 1978. Usually referred to as the Copyright Act of 1976, it is more formally known as Public Law 94-553, 90 Stat. 2541 (1976), Title 17 of the U.S. Code codified at 17 U.S.C. Sections 101-810. All references to section numbers are to this law. Its predecessor is referred to as the Copyright Act of 1909.

CREATION. "A work is 'created' when it is fixed in a copy or phonorecord for the first time; where a work is prepared over a period of time, the portion of it that has been fixed at any particular time constitutes the work as of that time, and where the work has been prepared in different versions, each version constitutes a separate work." [7]

DECLARATORY JUDGMENT. Action that determines whether the law is or is not violated under a particular set of facts.

DEFENDANT. The party against whom the legal action is brought; frequently the alleged copyright infringer.

DE MINIMUS. Insufficient injury to support a cause of action.

DERIVATIVE WORK. "A work based upon one or more preexisting works, such as a translation, musical arrangement, dramatization, fictionalization, motion picture version, sound recording, art reproduction, abridgment, condensation, or any other form in which a work may be recast, transformed, or adapted. A work consisting of editorial revisions, annotations, elaborations, or other modifications which, as a whole, represent an original work of authorship" (see also Chapter 3). [8]

DISPLAY. "To show a copy of [a work] either directly or by means of a film, slide, television image, or any other device or process or, in the case of a motion picture or other audiovisual work, to show individual images nonsequentially" (compare with **perform**; see also **publicly**). [9]

FIXED. "A work is 'fixed' in a tangible medium of expression when its embodiment in a copy or phonorecord, by or under the authority of the author, is sufficiently permanent or stable to permit it to be perceived, reproduced, or otherwise communicated for a period of more than transitory duration. A work consisting of sound, images, or both, that are being transmitted, is 'fixed' for purposes of this title if a fixation of the work is being made simultaneously with its transmission" (see also Chapter 3). [10]

INJUNCTION. Remedy granted by the court, at the request of the complainant, forbidding the defendant from doing some act. A **preliminary injunction** is a temporary injunction granted pending the outcome of litigation where the right to an injunction will be determined. A **permanent injunction** is granted when the right to an injunction is at issue and favorably decided. It may also be part of the relief granted by a final judgment.

LAW. See STATUTE.

LITERARY WORKS. "Works other than audiovisual works, expressed in words, numbers, or other verbal or numerical symbols or indicia, regardless of the nature of the material objects, such as books, periodicals, manuscripts, phonorecords, film, tapes, disks, or cards, in which they are embodied." [11]

MOTION PICTURES. "Audiovisual works consisting of a series of related images which, when shown in succession, impart an impression of motion, together with accompanying sounds, if any" (compare with **audiovisual works.** This seems to include musical videodisks). [12]

PERFORM. "To recite, render, play, dance, or act it, either directly or by means of any device or process or, in the case of a motion picture or other audiovisual work, to show its images in any sequence or to make the sound accompanying it audible" (compare with **display**; see also **publicly**). [13]

PERFORMING RIGHTS SOCIETIES. Refers to the three organizations that handle nondramatic musical performing rights: American Society of Composers, Authors, and Publishers (ASCAP); Broadcast Music, Inc. (BMI); and SESAC (formerly the Society of European Stage Authors and Composers).

PERMANENT INJUNCTION. See INJUNCTION.

PHONORECORDS. "Material objects in which sounds, other than those accompanying a motion picture or other audiovisual work, are fixed by any method now known or later developed, and from which the sounds can be perceived, reproduced, or otherwise communicated, either directly or with the aid of a machine or device. The term 'phonorecords' includes the material object in which the sounds are first fixed" (compare with **sound recordings**).[14]

PLAINTIFF. The party initiating the legal action, usually the copyright proprietor or a licensee.

PRELIMINARY INJUNCTION. See INJUNCTION.

PRODUCER. The person who puts together "the deal." That is, the person who finds and clears the rights to the literary property; employs the script writer(s), talent, and technicians; obtains financing; arranges distribution; and the like. [15]

PUBLICATION. "The distribution of copies or phonorecords of a work to the public by sale or other transfer of ownership, or by rental, lease, or lending. The offering to distribute copies or phonorecords to a group of persons for purposes of further distribution, public performance, or public display, constitutes publication. A public performance or display of a work does not of itself constitute publication." [16] In other words, projecting or exhibiting an audiovisual work in a theatre or by TV does not constitute a publication of the work. Distributing movie prints to theatres or TV stations does constitute publication. [17]

PUBLIC DOMAIN. Materials that are no longer or have never been under copyright protection.

REGULATION. An authoritative rule dealing with procedure having the force of law. Copyright regulations are issued by the Copyright Office, Copyright Royalty Tribunal, Customs Service, and other federal agencies (compare with **common law** and **statute**).

RELEASE. When the person in whom a right, claim, or privilege exists, relinquishes it to another, usually through a license or other written document.

SOUND RECORDINGS. "Works that result from the fixation of a series of musical, spoken, or other sounds, but not including the sounds accompanying a motion picture or other audiovisual work, regardless of the nature of the material objects, such as disks, tapes, or other phonorecords, in which they are embodied" (compare with **phonorecords**). [18]

STATUTE. A law enacted by the legislative branch of government and signed by the President (compare with **common law** and **regulation**).

SUMMARY JUDGMENT. The plaintiff or defendant in a civil action can move for summary judgment when that party desires a quick resolution of a complaint without a trial. The petition is based on the assumption that there is no genuine factual issue and that he or she is entitled to prevail.

TORT. A civil wrong other than breach of contract.

TRANSMIT. "To communicate [a performance or display] by any device or process whereby images or sounds are received beyond the place from which they are sent" (see also **display**). [19]

REFERENCES

1. Lewis Carroll, *Alice's Adventures in Wonderland and Through the Looking-Glass* (New York: Collier Books, 1962), p. 247.
2. The following works were helpful in establishing definitions: *Black's Law Dictionary*, 5th ed. (St. Paul: West Publishing Co., 1979); Esther R. Sinofsky, *Off-Air Videotaping in Education: Copyright Issues, Decisions, Implications* (New York: R. R. Bowker, 1984), pp. 127-129; and *Words and Phrases* (St. Paul: West, n.d.).
3. U.S., Congress, Senate, *An Act for the General Revision of the Copyright Law, Title 17 of the United States Code*, Pub. L. 94-553, 94th Cong., 2d sess., 1976, S.22, Section 101. Hereafter, all citations to a section number refer to this Copyright Act.
4. Section 101.
5. Section 101.
6. Section 101.
7. Section 101.
8. Section 101.
9. Section 101.
10. Section 101.
11. Section 101.
12. Section 101.
13. Section 101.
14. Section 101.
15. Los Angeles County Bar Association, Intellectual Property and Unfair Competition Section, *Producing for Motion Pictures and Television: A Practical Guide to Legal Issues*, ed. Vance Scott Van Petten (Beverly Hills: Los Angeles County Bar Association, 1983), p. v.
16. Section 101.
17. Dixon Q. Dern, "Outline: Copyright—Subject Matter and Formalities; Motion Pictures and Other Audiovisual Works," in *Copyright: Selected Practical Approaches to Protection and Enforcement*, ed. Paul D. Supnik, Margaret Saal, and David Carson (Beverly Hills: Los Angeles County Bar Association, 1984), p. 57.
18. Section 101.
19. Section 101.

CHAPTER 2:

BACKGROUND BRIEFING

Copyright originated in Renaissance Italy as a protection for authors and inventors. However, it actually functioned as a protection for printers rather than authors. Well into the nineteenth century, authors sold their manuscripts to printers for small sums and depended on their patrons' subsidies for survival.

Change slowly began in England in 1710 when Parliament enacted the Statute of Anne which vested copyright in the author not the publisher. As copyright became protection for the author, a new set of tensions arose, ones that are still with us: how to reconcile the interests of publishers, authors, and users. Critics claim this tie between copyright and printing pervades the 1976 Act and inhibits the passage of a copyright act reflecting the dynamics of the twentieth century marketplace.

From as early as Henry VIII's reign, copyright also operated as a religious and political censor. Printers obtained a copyright for a work through membership in the Stationers' Company and the Company only granted copyright to works acceptable to the Crown.

Copyright immigrated to the "13 colonies" along with other British customs and laws. The Statute of Anne was never effectively applied in America, but it became the model for early U.S. copyright legislation. A few of the colonies passed copyright laws and 12 of the 13 states passed state copyright laws during the Confederation period. Congress passed the first U.S. copyright act in 1790; revised it four times (in 1831, 1870, 1909, and 1976); and amended it frequently as societal, economic, and technological change demanded.

Congress' mandate to legislate copyright (and patents) stems from Article I, Section 8, Clause 8 of the U.S. Constitution: "To promote the progress of science and useful arts, by securing for limited times to authors and inventors the exclusive right to their respective writings and discoveries." Basically, this clause states that the purpose of copyright is to advance the public welfare. To accomplish this purpose, individuals are encouraged to create new works through the promise of economic reward. As the Supreme Court explained in *Sony v. Universal*: "The monopoly privileges that Congress may authorize are neither unlimited nor primarily designed to provide a special private benefit. Rather, the limited grant is a means by which an important public purpose may be achieved." [1]

But balancing copyright's purpose (providing public access to information) and the means to its accomplishment (monetary reward) has stymied Congress. Of the various suggested approaches for reconciling public access with economic reward, the two most accepted are **fair use** and the **idea-expression dichotomy**. Fair use allows someone to use a copyrighted work without the copyright owner's permission in a few, selected instances. (See Chapter 5 for a discussion of fair use.) The idea-expression dichotomy allows free use of a copyrighted work's ideas while restricting use of its expression. In *Landsberg v. Scrabble Crossword Game Players*, the Ninth Circuit maintained:

> [I]t is an axiom of copyright law that copyright protects only an author's expression of an idea and not the idea itself.... Corollary to this axiom is a strong policy permitting all to use freely the ideas contained in a copyrighted work so long as copyrighted expression is not appropriated. [2]

In other words, borrowing an idea may be tolerated (but beware of other laws such as unfair competition); plagiarism, never. Section 102 (discussed in Chapter 3) reflects this train of thought in defining what is copyrightable.

10

REFERENCES

1. 52 U.S.L.W. 4090, 4092-4093 (U.S. Jan. 17, 1984).
2. 221 U.S.P.Q. 1140, 1142 (9th Cir. 1984).

CHAPTER   3:

CAN   YOU   COPYRIGHT   IT?

You just completed a production. Can you copyright it?
Three sections of the 1976 Act govern the copyrightability of your
work: Sections 102, 103, and 105.

WHAT CAN BE COPYRIGHTED?

Section 102. Subject matter of copyright: In general

(a) Copyright protection subsists, in accordance with this
title, in original works of authorship fixed in any tangible
medium of expression, now known or later developed, from
which they can be perceived, reproduced, or otherwise
communicated, either directly or with the aid of a machine
or device. Works of authorship include the following
categories:
  (1) literary works;
  (2) musical works, including any accompanying words;
  (3) dramatic works, including any accompanying music;
  (4) pantomimes and choreographic works;
  (5) pictorial, graphic, and sculptural works;
  (6) motion pictures and other audiovisual works; and
  (7) sound recordings.
(b) In no case does copyright protection for an original work
of authorship extend to any idea, procedure, process,
system, method of operation, concept, principle, or dis-

covery, regardless of the form in which it is described, explained, illustrated, or embodied in such work. [1]

What Is Meant by Fixation?

In its analysis of subsection (a) of Section 102, Congress focused on the meanings of **fixation, original work,** and the specific categories. Congress noted the importance of fixation in distinguishing between common law and statutory protection. For example, "an improvisation or an unrecorded choreographic work, performance, or broadcast, would continue to be subject to protection under State common law or statute, but would not be eligible for federal statutory protection under Section 102." [2]

Section 301 returns to the distinctions between common law and statutory protection and between fixed and unfixed works. Its subsection (a) abolishes common law copyright for works not yet published and establishes a single federal system protecting published and unpublished fixed works. Subsection (b) delineates three areas excluded from subsection (a) and so preserved by the states. One of the three is subject matter outside the scope of Sections 102 and 103. Thus, fixation is a critical criterion for federal copyrightability.

The House also considered the definition of fixation as a way of resolving the status of live broadcasts (such as sports, news coverage, and live performances of music) that reach the public in unfixed form but are simultaneously being recorded. Taking a football game covered by a director and four camera operators for its example, the House opined that the crew's choice and sequencing of shots satisfied the requirements for authorship. But what about fixation? If transmitted live and simultaneously recorded, the game qualified for statutory protection. [3]

What is Meant by Original Work?

The House distinguished an original work from "the multitude of material objects in which it can be embodied." [4] Thus a book, for example, is not a work of authorship, but a type of **copy**. In other words, an author writes a **literary work**. That work can then be embodied in a wide range of copies; that is, in books, microfilm, computer punch cards, and the like.

The Categories of Authorship

Original works fall into one of the seven categories listed in Section 102(a). While the scope of each of the seven categories for works of authorship may appear self-evident, Congress defined four of them in Section 101 (see Chapter 1) and further clarified their meaning when discussing the bill that became the 1976 Copyright Act. For example:

- **Sound recordings** are "[t]he aggregation of sounds and not the tangible medium of fixation." **Phonorecords** are "the physical objects in which sounds are fixed." [5]

- **Sound tracks** are included within motion pictures, not sound recordings.

- **Motion pictures** require three characteristics: (1) a series of images (2) capable of being shown in successive order and (3) giving the impression of motion when shown. This includes film, tape, and other media, but excludes such items as unauthorized fixations of live performances or telecasts and live telecasts not fixed simultaneously with transmission. Filmstrips and slide sets are excluded because they do not meet the impression-of-motion criterion.

- **Audiovisual works** such as filmstrips, slide sets, and transparencies are equated with motion pictures and not pictorial works.

- **Literary works** does not refer to literary merit. "It includes catalogs, directories and similar works." [6] In fact, any work that does not fit into one of the other six categories is considered a literary work. This includes such works as soup-can labels, decorative lamp shades, and fabric patterns.

What Cannot Be Copyrighted?

Chapter 2 introduced the idea-expression dichotomy as a possible solution to the problem of balancing public access to information with economic reward to the creator. The purpose of Section 102(b) "is to restate . . . that the basic dichotomy between expression and idea remains unchanged" by the 1976 Act. [7] Copyright Office Circulars R31, R32, and R34, reproduced in Appendices D1-D3 respectively, show how the Copyright Office explicated this subsection.

In *A. A. Hoehling v. Universal City Studios*, the plaintiff claimed that Michael Mooney's book *The Hindenburg* and Universal's picture by the same name, based in part on the book, infringed his 1962 book, *Who Destroyed the Hindenburg?* Hoehling researched the 1937 disaster seeking to prove the sabotage theory raised by the official investigation. Mooney's somewhat fictionalized account also pushed the sabotage angle as did the movie. The defendants contended that their works were only similar to the plaintiff's in respect to the historical facts which are not copyrightable. District Judge Metzner agreed with the defendants:

Although the facts . . . are the product of plaintiff's lengthy research and marshalling, they and the theory for which they form the base are not copyrightable. If they were, we would not have a plethora of writing about who wrote Shakespeare's plays, or who killed John F. Kennedy. [8]

The judge granted the defendants' motion for summary judgment.

Since an idea is not copyrightable, how can you protect a production idea until you develop it? One way is to develop a written treatment, a brief synopsis including character and action development of any production ideas you may have. The treatment may be copyrighted, thus protecting your expression of the idea. [9] In California, the "law allows for recovery for the breach of an implied-in-fact contract when the recipient of a valuable idea accepts the information knowing that compensation is expected, and subsequently used the idea without paying for it." But if you disclose the idea before demanding payment as a condition for use, no implied contract exists. [10]

COPYRIGHTING COMPILATIONS AND DERIVATIVE WORKS

While Section 102 discusses copyrightability in general terms, Section 103 zeroes in on two potential problem areas—compilations and derivative works.

> Section 103. Subject matter of copyright: Compilations and derivative works
>
> (a) The subject matter of copyright as specified by section 102 includes compilations and derivative works, but protection for a work employing preexisting material in which copyright subsists does not extend to any part of the work in which such material has been used unlawfully. (b) The copyright in a compilation or derivative work extends only to the material contributed by the author of such work, as distinguished from the preexisting material employed in the work, and does not imply any exclusive right in the preexisting material. The copyright in such work is independent of, and does not affect or enlarge the scope, duration, ownership, or subsistence of, any copyright protection in the preexisting material. [11]

Compilations result "from a process of selecting, bringing together, organizing, and arranging previously existing material of all kinds, regardless of whether the individual items in the material have been or ever could have been subject to copyright." [12] **Derivative works** involve recasting, transforming, or adapting a preexisting work or works. The underlying work must qualify under Section 102 regardless of whether it is or has ever been copyrighted (see Chapter 4 for a fuller treatment of derivative works).

The most important point here is one that is commonly misunderstood today: Copyright in a "new version" covers only the material added by the later author, and has no effect one way or the other on the copyright or public domain status of the preexisting material. [13]

For example, if you copyright an annotated version of Shakespeare's *Romeo and Juliet*, the copyright would only cover your annotations. The play remains in the public domain. Similarly, the composer of "A Fifth of Beethoven" received copyright protection only for the additions to Beethoven's *Fifth Symphony*. [14] But, although the original work (literary work, motion picture, etc.) may be in the public domain, and copyright applies only to the second edition, the entire work must be treated as a copyrighted work—unless the public domain elements can be clearly identified (see Chapters 13 and 15 for further discussion of music and public domain works).

COPYRIGHTABILITY OF GOVERNMENT WORKS

Section 105 places an abundance of materials into the public domain. For you, the producer, it may translate into big savings and less trouble if you can use these materials rather than copyrighted ones which require permission—and often payment—for use.

Section 105. Subject matter of copyright: United States government works

Copyright protection under this title is not available for any work of the United States Government, but the United States Government is not precluded from receiving and holding copyrights transferred to it by assignment, bequest, or otherwise. [15]

However, if you are an independent contractor producing materials for a U.S. government agency, the question arises of whether you may obtain a private copyright for your work. Each government agency determines whether an independent contractor may copyright a work prepared in whole or part with government funds. Congress assumed that a work commissioned for an agency's own use (that is, instead of having an employee do it) would not be copyrightable. It saw other situations where the lack of copyrightability would hamper the production of important works. So in negotiating your government contract, clarify the copyrightability of your finished product.

Schnapper v. Foley tested Congress' intent in Section 105. M. B. Schnapper, editor of Public Affairs press, sought an injunction invalidating the copyright to a film series about the Supreme Court entitled *Equal Justice Under Law*. The series was commissioned by the Administrative Office of the U.S. Courts (of which William E. Foley was the director). Schnapper also asked the court to prohibit federal agencies from allowing such copyrights in the future. In reaching its decision, the court considered the legislative intent of Section 105 and concluded that the series' copyright was valid. [16]

This section also impacts copyright transfer forms; that is, the written transfer of copyright most publishers require as a condition of acceptance for publication. Many transfer forms now include a signature block for U.S. government authors only. If your forms do not allow for this variation, the U.S. Department of Commerce recommended the following statement to its personnel: "This is to certify that the article named above was prepared by a United States Government employee(s) as part of his (her) (their) official duties and is therefore a work of the U.S. Government and not subject to copyright." [17]

Two limitations apply to Section 105: (1) It does not apply to works created by U.S. Postal Service employees; i.e., stamps, and (2) it only applies to works written by U.S. Government employees within the scope of their official duties.

REFERENCES

1. Section 102.
2. U.S., Congress, House, Committee on the Judiciary, *Copyright Law Revision*, H. Rept. No. 94-1476, 94th Cong., 2d sess., 1976, p. 52; U.S., Congress, Senate, Committee on the Judiciary, *Copyright Law Revision*, S. Rept. No. 94-473, 94th Cong., 1st sess., 1975, p. 51. Hereafter, all citations to these reports will be referred to as *House* and *Senate* respectively. When the reports use identical wording, both references are given.
3. *House*, p. 52.
4. *House*, p. 52.
5. *Senate*, p. 53; *House*, p. 56.
6. *Senate*, p. 53; *House*, pp. 53-54.
7. *Senate*, p. 54; *House*, p. 57.
8. Copyright L. Rep. (CCH) ¶25,096 (S.D.N.Y. 1979), p. 15,549.
9. E. Leonard Rubin, "Film and Video and the Law," in *Law & the Arts—Arts & the Law* (Chicago: Lawyers for the Creative Arts, 1979), p. 71.
10. *Landsberg v. Scrabble Crossword Game Players, Inc.*, 231 U.S.P.Q. 658 (9th Cir. 1986).
11. Section 103.
12. *Senate*, p. 55; *House*, p. 57.
13. *Senate*, p. 55; *House*, p. 57.
14. Joseph Taubman, *In Tune with the Music Business* (New York: Law-Arts Publishers, 1980), pp. 22-23.
15. Section 105.
16. 202 U.S.P.Q. 699 (D.D.C. 1979).
17. U.S., Department of Commerce, National Bureau of Standards, Administrative Bulletin 78-28, June 19, 1978.

CHAPTER 4:

COPYRIGHT OWNERSHIP AND RIGHTS

Once you determine that your product can be copyrighted (see Chapter 3), you need to identify the copyright owner. Do you own the copyright on the product or does your employer or client own it? If you are the copyright owner, what rights do you have? Or, if you want to use someone else's copyrighted work, what rights does that person own?

Sections 201 and 106 cover copyright ownership and the rights granted with it.

WHO OWNS THE COPYRIGHT

Section 201. Ownership of copyright

(a) INITIAL OWNERSHIP.—Copyright in a work protected under this title vests initially in the author or authors of the work. The authors of a joint work are coowners of copyright in the work.

(b) WORKS MADE FOR HIRE.—In the case of a work made for hire, the employer or other person for whom the work was prepared is considered the author for purposes of this title, and, unless the parties have expressly agreed otherwise in a written instrument signed by them, owns all of the rights comprised in the copyright.[1]

Initial Ownership

Subsection (a) restates two well-established principles of copyright law: (1) the source of ownership is the work's author; and, (2) coauthors of a joint work are coowners of the copyright. In its discussion of **joint work,** Congress explained:

> The touchstone here is intention, at the time the writing is done, that the parts to be absorbed or combined into an integrated unit, although the parts themselves may be either "inseparable" (as the case of a novel or painting) or "interdependent" (as in the case of a motion picture, opera, or the words and music of a song). The definition of "joint work" is to be contrasted with the definition of "collective work" ... in which the elements of merger and unity are lacking; there the key elements are assemblage or gathering . . . . [2]

Works Made for Hire

Subsection (b) adopts one of the basic principles of the 1909 Copyright Act: when a work is made for hire, the employer is considered the author, that is, the initial copyright owner. It also requires a signed, written agreement if the employee is to own any rights.

The definition of **work made for hire** gave Congress some trouble. After extensive revision, the following two-part definition was included in Section 101:

(1) A work prepared by an employee within the scope of his or her employment; or

(2) A work specially ordered or commissioned for use as a contribution to a collective work, as a part of a motion picture or other audiovisual work, as a translation, as a

supplementary work, as a compilation, as an instructional text, as a test, as answer material for a test, or as an atlas, if the parties expressly agree in a written instrument signed by them that the work shall be considered a work made for hire. For the purpose of the foregoing sentence, a "supplementary work" is a work prepared for publication as a secondary adjunct to a work by another author for the purpose of introducing, concluding, illustrating, explaining, revising, commenting upon, or assisting in the use of the other work, such as forewords, afterwords, pictorial illustrations, maps, charts, tables, editorial notes, musical arrangements, answer material for tests, bibliographies, appendixes, and indexes, and an "instructional text" is a literary, pictorial, or graphic work prepared for publication and with the purpose of use in systematic instructional activities.[3]

Part (1) of the definition means that works prepared by an in-house instructional design or production group belong to the institution, organization, or company employing the group.

Part (2) lists nine specific categories of commissioned works that may be considered as made for hire: (a) a contribution to a collective work; (b) part of a motion picture or other audiovisual work; (c) a translation; (d) a supplementary work; (e) a compilation; (f) an instructional text; (g) a test; (h) answer material for a test; and, (i) an atlas. According to Congress:

Of these, one of the most important categories is that of "instructional texts." This term is given its own definition in the bill: "a literary, pictorial, or graphic work prepared for publication with the purpose of use in systematic instructional activities." The concept is intended to include what might loosely be called "textbook materials," whether or not in book form or prepared in the form of text matter. The basic characteristic of "instructional texts" is the purpose of their preparation for "use in systematic instructional activities," and they are to be distinguished from works prepared for use by a general readership. 4

In addition, Part (2) affects the contracts of free-lancers because it stipulates that the concerned parties agree in writing "that the work shall be considered a work made for hire." So if you hire an outside consultant, include a work-for-hire agreement in the contract in order to retain the copyright. Similarly, if you are an independent contractor, carefully check the contract's statement of the agreement.

You should also watch legislative developments in this area. At the federal level, bills such as S. 2138 and H.R. 5911 (introduced in 1984) attempt to amend the Copyright Law's definition of a work made for hire. If enacted, such bills could affect the types of works considered made for hire, the types of rights granted free-lancers, the withholding of federal payroll taxes, and the payment of Social Security taxes.

At the state level, the definition of work made for hire has already been affected. For example, a 1982 California law amended the definition of **employee** in the state's Workers' Compensation Act and that of **employer** in its Unemployment Insurance Code. As a result, those commissioning works made for hire may find themselves liable for (1) maintaining workers' compensation insurance coverage for outside contractors; (2) any injuries sustained by this employee during the course of the contracted work; and, (3) contributions to the state's unemployment insurance and disability insurance funds. [NOTE: Sections 201(c)-205 are not discussed as they deal with ownership and transfer of ownership concepts beyond the scope of this primer.] 5

COPYRIGHT OWNER'S RIGHTS

While Section 201 identifies the copyright owner, Section 106 lists the rights granted that owner.

Section 106.   Exclusive rights in copyrighted works

Subject to sections 107 through 118, the owner of copyright under this title has the exclusive rights to do and to authorize any of the following:

(1) to reproduce the copyrighted work in copies or phonorecords;

(2) to prepare derivative works based upon the copyrighted work;

(3) to distribute copies or phonorecords of the copyrighted work to the public by sale or other transfer of ownership, or by rental, lease, or lending;

(4) in the case of literary, musical, dramatic, and choreographic works, pantomimes, and motion pictures and other audiovisual works, to perform the copyrighted work publicly; and

(5) in the case of literary, musical, dramatic, and choreographic works, pantomimes, and pictorial, graphic, or sculptural works, including the individual images of a motion picture or other audiovisual work, to display the copyrighted work publicly. [6]

This section grants copyright owners five fundamental rights: (1) reproduction; (2) adaptation; (3) publication; (4) public performance; and, (5) public display.   These five exclusive rights comprise the "bundle of rights" that is a copyright.   They are subject to the limitations imposed by Sections 107 through 118.   Derivative works and the definition of **publicly** in Sections 106(4) and (5) require special attention.

Derivative Works

As defined in Chapter 1 and restated in Chapter 3, a **derivative work** is a work based upon a preexisting work.   Examples include translations, musical arrangements, motion pictures based on a book or script, books based on motion pictures, editorial revisions, and annotations.   The copyright on these works extends only to the new material contributed. The copyright or public domain status of the underlying work is not changed.

Section 106(2) means you need the copyright owner's permission to "do something" with a copyrighted work whether it is producing a motion picture or TV series based on a novel or laying down a musical sound track or designing a student guide for a specific textbook.

Consider the case of Melaim Lenoir King, an economics teacher who prepared brief, one-page outlines of the day's key points for the students who came to him for tutoring. The outlines, for which there was no charge, were always collected and destroyed. In 1914, Macmillan, the publisher of the textbook upon which the outline was based, sued for copyright infringement. The publisher maintained the outlines were unauthorized, unfair, and unlawful abridgments of the textbook. King claimed his outlines were typical of materials customarily prepared by teachers for students and, therefore, not an infringement.

The court differentiated between King's outlines and other such outlines on the basis of how much of the book's expression had been reproduced. According to the court, King appropriated more of the textbook's ideas and language then permitted by copyright. And, despite the "incomplete and fragmentary" nature of King's appropriation, "important portions of them are left substantially recognizable" as the ideas and language of the original work. Had King's outlines merely referred to the book for a particular topic without reproducing so much of its information, then they "might have been considered study aids without substantial reproduction."[7]

Therefore, the court concluded that King's outlines were abridgments he had no right to make. "They constitute 'versions' of substantial portions of the book, such as the plaintiff alone has the right to make." [8] Furthermore, the court explained that it was

unable to believe that the defendant's use of the outlines is any the less infringement of the copyright because he is a teacher, because he uses them in teaching the contents of the book, because he might lecture upon the contents of the book without infringing, or because his pupils might have taken their own notes of his lecture without infringing.[9]

As a final note, the court pointed out that the outlines could harm the sale of the book if students thought they could rely on the outlines and save money by not buying the book.

Section 106(2) also means problems for a producer if the copyright owner decides to terminate the rights granted the producer vis-a-vis production and distribution of the derivative work. Such problems with underlying works forced many motion pictures out of release; for example, *Thanks for the Memory* (1938 with Bob Hope), *You Can't Take It With You* (1938 with Jean Arthur, James Stewart, and Lionel Barrymore), and *The Man Who Came to Dinner* (1942 with Monty Woolley). [10]

Jaszi identified four ways conflicts arise between a film and its underlying work:

(1) The motion picture was granted only limited rights.

(2) When the production company was sold, the film's copyright was bought but not the rights in the underlying work.

(3) Under the 1909 Act, the copyright owner's heirs did not have to reassign any rights to the derivative work at renewal time (see also Section 304(a) of the 1976 Act).

(4) The underlying work is still copyrighted but the film entered the public domain—usually because someone forgot to renew the copyright. [11]

The first type of conflict usually occurs when the underlying work is an independent creation such as a novel or play. It is least likely to occur when the scripts, musical scores, and the like, are created specifically for the film; especially when they are considered works made for hire and thus under the producer's copyright ownership.

In *Goodis v. United Artists Television*, the executors of David Goodis' estate brought a copyright infringement action against UA Television and the American Broadcasting Companies (ABC) claiming UA's TV series "The Fugitive" broadcast by ABC infringed the copyright of Goodis' novel *Dark Passage*. In 1945, Goodis sold exclusive motion picture rights in the novel to Warner Brothers for $25,000. The contract included clauses to cover radio and TV broadcast rights. The question, according to the Second Circuit, was whether the contract conveyed to Warner Brothers the right to create a TV series such as "The Fugitive." The district court concluded that the contract clearly conveyed the right to produce a film series like "The Fugitive" and thus decreed a summary judgment for the defendants. The circuit court disagreed. Two of the judges held that Goodis retained certain rights in his novel's characters and therefore reversed and remanded the case for further proceedings. [12]

In *Gilliam v. ABC*, the plaintiffs prevented ABC from broadcasting a compilation of "Monty Python's Flying Circus" episodes it wanted to edit. One reason the court granted the requested injunction was that the plaintiffs had not consented to the changes ABC proposed. The court saw the changes as an infringement of common law copyright in unpublished episode scripts. [13]

The third type of conflict between derivative and underlying works—the heirs do not reassign rights—is exemplified by cases such as *Rohauer v. Killiam Shows, Inc.* and *The Harry Fox Agency v. Mills Music, Inc.*

Rohauer concerned Rudolph Valentino's 1926 film *The Son of the Sheik* which was based on Edith M. Hull's copyrighted novel, *The Sons of the Sheik*. Hull granted the film an unlimited and unconditional license to use her novel. Her legal heirs to the novel's copyright wanted to prevent continued use of the film, despite Hull's unlimited license, under the concept of "new estate." Under new estate, the heirs to a copyright could terminate the license granted by the original owner at renewal time. (The 1909 Act issued the original copyright for 28 years, renewable for 28 more years.) The court found that ownership of the copyright renewal did not have to effect the film's continued use. In other words, derivative works can be independent. [14]

The Harry Fox Agency v. Mills Music was an interpleader action (that is, a proceeding to determine a right on which the action of a third party depends) to resolve a dispute over the 1920s copyrighted song, "Who's Sorry Now," written by Tom Snyder, Burt Kalman, and Harry Ruby. Snyder's widow and son, the statutory copyright heirs, used Section 304 of the 1976 Act to terminate the grant to Mills Music. Mills claimed it was still entitled to royalties; the Snyders said, "Not so." The Harry Fox Agency, which issued licenses and collected various royalties for the song, took the matter to court so it could properly distribute the royalties.

The district court concluded that authors and composers were given the right to terminate previously made grants in order to recapture lost benefits. But, this is subject to an exception for derivative works such as sound recordings of a copyrighted song. Under this exception, the grant's terms may continue after termination. Thus, Mills was entitled to royalties. [15]

The Second Circuit did not agree. It characterized the case as presenting "a novel question of considerable importance concerning the meaning and application of the 'derivative works exception' to the termination of transfers provision of the Copyright Act of 1976 [Section 304]." And declared that it was "required to reverse" because it believed "the scales tip in favor of the author's heirs, and that the music publisher/middleman, having already had the benefit of a renewal term, is without recourse upon termination." [16] The court also commented on the limitations placed by Section 107-118 on Section 106 rights:

> These limitations are imposed to vindicate the public interest in the need for access to information contained in copyrighted works and in the promotion of a multiplicity of voices in society. The derivative works exception guarantees public access to derivative works . . . by withholding from the owner of the underlying copyright after termination a veto power over continued utilization of these works. [17]

The case was appealed to the U.S. Supreme Court which granted certiorari, that is, agreed to hear the case, on March 26, 1984. As of this writing, the Supreme Court has not handed down its decision.

The fourth type of conflict focuses on derivative works entering the public domain while their underlying works are still protected by copyright. Films in the public domain include *Till the Clouds Roll By, It's a Wonderful Life, The Stranger, Life With Father, Santa Fe Trail, A Farewell to Arms, Meet John Doe, The Third Man,* and *My Man Godfrey* (but remember, the underlying works may still be copyrighted). [18] Three cases addressing this issue are *Classic Film Museum v. Warner Brothers, Cyril Russell v. Daniel A. Price,* and *Filmvideo Releasing Corporation v. Hastings.*

Classic Film Museum dealt with a public domain film and an unpublished screenplay. In 1953, Warner Brothers acquired the copyright to the 1937 version of *A Star Is Born* but failed to renew the copyright in 1965. Thus the movie entered the public domain.

Classic Film Museum distributed films to TV and nontheatrical users. Warner Brothers claimed that the Classic Film Museum's rentals of the film infringed its common law copyright in the unpublished screenplay, story, and musical score. The trial court ruled that the film could be freely used without Warner Brothers' permission. In affirming this ruling, the First Circuit asserted:

> The owner of a common-law copyright in the underlying work cannot expand the statutorily created monopoly, the limitation of which is designed to place in the public domain not only the copyrighted matter but also the good will generated throughout the period of the monopoly. [19]

Otherwise, a conflict would arise between the Constitution's limited monopoly policy (Article I, Section 8, Clause 8) and the Copyright Act itself (but compare with *Gilliam* discussed earlier and *Russell* discussed next).

In *Russell*, the defendants distributed copies of the film version of *Pygmalion* which had entered the public domain in 1966. They were sued by the owners of the copyright renewal in the George Bernard Shaw play upon which the film was based. The defendants argued that the film's copyright had expired, placing it in the public domain; consequently, prints of the film could be used freely by anyone. [20]

Affirming the lower court's grant of damages and attorney fees to the plaintiffs (approximately $13,700), the Ninth Circuit maintained

> [T]he well-established doctrine that a derivative copyright protects only the new material contained in the derivative work, not the matter derived from the underlying work.... Thus, although the derivative work may enter the public domain, the matter contained therein which derives from a work still covered by statutory copyright is not dedicated to the public .... The established doctrine prevents un-authorized copying or other infringing use of the underlying work or any part of that work contained in the derivative product so long as the underlying work itself remains copyrighted. [21]

Thus the plaintiffs could prevent the defendants from renting the film for unauthorized exhibition.

The Ninth Circuit also explained that *Classic Film Museum v. Warner Brothers* did not apply here because there the underlying work was under common-law copyright which would have given indefinite protection at odds with copyright's limited monopoly concept. Thus *A Star Is Born* could be exhibited without infringing the underlying work.

In 1976, Filmvideo Releasing Corporation brought action against David R. Hastings, II, the administrator of Clarence E. Mulford's estate, "for declaratory judgment that renewal copyrights are invalid or motion pictures are in public domain." [22] The defendants counterclaimed for an injunction and copyright infringement damages. The renewal copyrights in question were those for seventeen "Hopalong Cassidy" books Mulford wrote and copyrighted between 1907 and 1935. The motion pictures in question were seventeen Hopalong Cassidy films Paramount Pictures produced and copyrighted under agreement with Mulford. The films' copyrights expired in the 1960s. "The issue is whether the defendants' renewal copyrights *in the novels* [emphasis in original] may be infringed by the showing on television of motion pictures now in the public domain which were made under an agreement with the author." [23] The district court decided that the books' renewal copyrights "can be infringed by the use of materials in the public domain as readily as they are by the use of separately copyrighted matter." [24] None of the motions for judgment were granted.

Legal action recommenced in 1981 when the plaintiff requested a declaratory judgment permitting it to license twenty-three Hopalong Cassidy motion pictures for TV exhibition. The defendants counterclaimed seeking injunctive relief and copyright infringement damages. The district court found that the motion pictures infringed on the books and enjoined Filmvideo from using or licensing any of the films for TV or home viewing via cassettes. [25]

On appeal to the Second Circuit, the district court's ruling was affirmed. The circuit court restated the principal question: "Whether a licensed, derivative copyrighted work and the underlying copyrighted matter which is [sic] incorporates both fall into the public domain where the underlying copyright has been renewed but the derivative copyright has not." The answer: "We agree with the Ninth Circuit, *Russell v. Price* . . . that the answer is 'No.' " [26]

As you can see (and will see in cases discussed later), the courts are not always consistent. When this occurs, a U.S. Supreme Court decision is usually needed to clarify the legal concepts involved. The Supreme Court, however, has denied certiorari to several of the cases already discussed. Pending action by the Supreme Court, the following conclusions may perhaps be drawn from these cases: If the copyright in the underlying work extends copyright protection beyond the term set by law and thus denies public access, a derivative work in the public domain may be used without authorization. Conversely, if the copyright in the underlying work is limited to the statutory term of copyright protection, the derivative work in the public domain may not be used without authorization lest copyright owners be denied their right to profit from their labors.

WHAT IS PUBLICLY?

Derivative works are not the only problem encountered in Section 106. What is meant by **publicly** in Sections 106(4) and (5)? Section 101 defined **publicly** as follows:

(1) to perform or display [a work] at a place open to the public or at any place where a substantial number of persons outside of a normal circle of a family and its social acquaintances is gathered; or
(2) to transmit or otherwise communicate a performance or display of the work to a place specified by clause (1) or to the public, by means of any device or process, whether the members of the public capable of receiving the performance or display receive it in the same place or in separate places and at the same time or at different times. [27]

In its discussion of Section 106, Congress defined *publicly* as "performance in 'semipublic' places such as clubs, lodges, factories, summer camps, and schools" and subject to copyright control. [28] Clubs and lodges include private clubs, country clubs, fraternal organizations, and the like. Limited membership is not a factor in defining publicly. [29] Similarly, "a performance or display in a university class is 'public' even if members of the general public are not admitted." [30] A 1984 Department of Defense directive provided the following guidelines for determining whether a performance is public: a performance in a residential facility (or a physical extension thereof) or an isolated area or deployed unit is not considered a public performance. If admission is charged, it normally would be considered a public performance. [31]

The California and Louisiana Attorney Generals disagreed on whether correctional facilities are considered "public." In California, the Director of Corrections asked: "Does the showing of videocassette tapes of motion pictures ['home use'-type tapes] to prison inmates by correctional authorities constitute an infringement of copyright?" The Attorney General's office answered: "The showing of videocassette tapes of motion pictures to prison inmates by correctional authorities without authorization from the copyright owner constitutes an infringement of copyright."[32]

In Louisiana, the Attorney General's office counseled its Department of Corrections that the once a month showing of rented videocassettes to 20-30 inmates is allowable. The opinion also took exception to the California opinion's definition of public performance: If a business meeting of 20-30 people is not considered public, then a correctional facility closed to the public should be so considered. [33]

Which opinion is right? The California Attorney General's answer appears to be the correct approach to the issue when viewed in the light of *Columbia Pictures Industries v. State of Wisconsin Department of Health and Social Services*. The plaintiffs in this case were nine major motion picture production and distribution companies: Columbia Pictures, Embassy Pictures, MGM/UA Entertainment, Paramount Pictures, Twentieth Century-Fox Film, United Artists, Universal City Studios, Walt Disney, and Warner Brothers. These companies license the right "to perform their copyrighted motion pictures publicly in several markets including theaters, pay cable, television networks and local television stations on college campuses, in hospitals, hotels and, relevant to this litigation, in correctional institutions."[34] They also manufacture videocassette copies of their copyrighted movies. These cassettes are sold to retailers who then sell and rent them to members of the public for showing at home. Members of the public.

> may perform the cassettes in their homes to a normal circle of their family and social acquaintances, but may not perform the cassettes in any manner which would infringe the exclusive rights under copyright to perform such motion pictures publicly. [35]

The case focused on practices at the Waupun Correctional Institution (WCI). In 1981, WCI installed a closed circuit TV system enabling inmates to connect their TV sets to a central antenna for viewing free TV broadcasts. In 1982, videocassette playback equipment was added to the closed circuit system giving WCI the ability to transmit videocassette performances to inmates. WCI then began renting and performing the plaintiffs' movies via the closed circuit TV system without authorization or license fee payments. Before this, the defendants had obtained licenses to publicly perform copyrighted motion pictures (in 16 or 35mm format) at WCI.

The court found that the defendants had publicly performed the plaintiffs' movies without authorization:

> Defendants' unauthorized transmission and performances of motion pictures copyrighted by plaintiffs over a closed circuit television system to inmates at WCI constitute infringements of plaintiffs' exclusive rights under copyright which have caused damage to each plaintiff. [36]

Therefore the court permanently prohibited the Department of Health and Social Services from further unauthorized transmissions or other public performances of the plaintiffs' movies in facilities under its supervision.

But why is the definition of publicly important to you? Money and/or permissions! A work publicly performed or displayed can command payment. If you are the copyright owner, you want to earn what is rightfully yours. You also may want to limit the use of your work. If you perform or display another's work, you must obtain permission and/or arrange payment for the use of that work. Exceptions are discussed in Chapters 5 and 6.

REFERENCES

1. Section 201.
2. *Senate*, pp. 103-104; *House*, p. 120.
3. Section 101.
4. *Senate*, p. 105; *House*, p. 121.
5. For more on this topic see, for example, Lionel S. Sobel, "A Practical Guide to Copyright Ownership and Transfer: The Difference Between Licenses, Assignments and Works Made for Hire," in *Copyright: Selected Practical Approaches to Protection and Enforcement*, pp. 41-47.
6. Section 106.
7. *Macmillan Co. v. King*, 18 Copy. Dec. 268, 273 (D.Mass. 1914).
8. *Macmillan*, p. 274.
9. *Macmillan*, p. 275.
10. Peter Jaszi, "When Works Collide: Derivative Motion Pictures, Underlying Rights, and the Public Interest," *UCLA Law Review* 28 (April 1981): 739-740.
11. Jaszi, pp. 750-753.
12. 425 F.2d 397 (2d Cir. 1970).
13. 538 F.2d 14 (2d Cir. 1976).
14. 379 F. Supp. 723 (S.D.N.Y. 1975), *rev'd*, 551 F.2d 484 (2d Cir. 1977).
15. 214 U.S.P.Q. 871 (S.D.N.Y. 1982).
16. 222 U.S.P.Q. 279, 281 (2d Cir. 1983).
17. *The Harry Fox Agency*, 1983, p. 288.
18. Jaszi, p. 765; *Sony*, p. 4096.
19. 202 U.S.P.Q. 467, 468 (1st Cir. 1979).
20. 448 F. Supp. 303 (C.D. Cal. 1977).
21. Copyright L. Rep. (CCH) ¶25,125 (9th Cir. 1979), pp. 15,741-15,742.
22. 193 U.S.P.Q. 305, 305 (S.D.N.Y. 1976).
23. *Filmvideo*, p. 306.
24. *Filmvideo*, p. 308.

25. *Filmvideo*, 212 U.S.P.Q. 195 (S.D.N.Y. 1981).
26. *Filmvideo*, Copyright L. Rep. (CCH) ¶25,339 (2d Cir. 1981), pp. 16,912-16,913.
27. Section 101.
28. *Senate*, p. 60; *House*, p. 64.
29. Bernard Korman, "Music Performance Rights," in *Current Developments in Copyright 1979* (New York: Practising Law Institute, 1979), pp. 191-192.
30. Robert W. Harris, "Memorandum: Introductory Guide to Academic Risks of Copyright Infringement," *The Journal of College and University Law* 7 (1980-81): 334.
31. U.S., Department of Defense, Directive Number 5535.4, 31 August 1984.
32. 65 Ops. Cal. Atty. Gen. 106 (1982).
33. "Showing Video Cassettes to Prisoners Is 'Fair Use,' " *PTCJ* 29 (7 March 1985): 480-481.
34. Civil Action No. 83-C-1496-R (E.D.Wis. Jan. 21, 1985), p. 2.
35. Civil Action No. 83-C-1496-R, p. 2.
36. Civil Action No. 83-C-1496-R, p. 4.

CHAPTER 5:

FAIR USE

The exclusive rights granted the copyright owner in Section 106 (see Chapter 4) are limited by the provisions in Sections 107 through 118. Of these limitations, Section 107, the fair use provision, is often the most misunderstood. Fair use is NOT educational use. Teaching does not automatically qualify as a justification for the unauthorized use of someone else's copyrighted material (see *Macmillan v. King* discussed in Chapter 4). Conversely, copying a small part of a work in a for-profit setting may be a form of fair use.

As a producer, you must be wary when applying the fair use doctrine. There are times when fair use will justify your use of a copyrighted work. But, you may find these times are far less frequent then you would wish. Fair use deals with your duplication of another's copyrighted work without permission AND to someone else's unauthorized duplication of your copyrighted materials—in certain circumstances. It is not blank permission to copy at will for worthwhile purposes.

This chapter provides a general overview of fair use. Specific cases are also discussed in Part II with their respective topics.

THE DOCTRINE OF FAIR USE

Section 107. Limitations on exclusive rights: Fair use

Notwithstanding the provisions of section 106, the fair use of a copyrighted work, including such use by reproduction in copies of phonorecords or by any other means specified by that section, for purposes such as criticism, comment, news reporting, teaching (including multiple copies for classroom use), scholarship, or research is not an infringement of copyright. In determining whether the use made of a work in any particular case is a fair use the factors to be considered shall include—

(1) the purpose and character of the use, including whether such use is of a commercial nature or is for nonprofit educational purposes;

(2) the nature of the copyrighted work;

(3) the amount and substantiality of the portion used in relation to the copyrighted work as a whole; and

(4) the effect of the use upon the potential market for or value of the copyrighted work. [1]

Fair use has no real definition. It is an equitable rule of reason the courts developed to help balance a copyright owner's exclusive rights with the public's need for information. Each case is judged on its own facts.

Congress intended Section 107 as a restatement of "the present judicial doctrine of fair use [and] not to change, narrow, or enlarge it in any way." [2] But, by adding teaching, scholarship, and research to the list of possible fair use purposes mentioned in Section 107, Congress may indeed have enlarged the scope of the doctrine. Criticism, comment, and news reporting are traditionally considered fair uses supported by the First Amendment. Teaching, scholarship, and research—all broad, education-related purposes not necessarily covered under the First Amendment—were included after intensive lobbying efforts. Previously, the courts did not recognize teaching as a justification for substantial copying (for example, *Macmillan v. King* and *Withol v. Crow*)—and they still do not recognize it (see *Marcus v. Rowley* discussed in Chapter 14).

EDUCATIONAL FAIR USE GUIDELINES

Guidelines for educational fair use for print and music were incorporated into the 1976 House report on the copyright bill; those for off-air taping were not ready until 1981 (see Appendix C for full text of guidelines). Congressionally-supported guidelines for other types of audiovisual works, such as computer software, have yet to appear.

Two basic problems exist regarding these guidelines: (1) They are not "the law." Being read into the *Congressional Record* or reproduced in a committee report is not the same as being incorporated into an act passed by Congress. As they now stand, the guidelines offer the courts—if they wish—a view of Congress' legislative intent. (2) Some educators and some producers have repudiated the guidelines. How this effects the application of the guidelines is not clear. [3]

These guidelines, however, do not appear to apply to commercially-produced educational materials or such materials produced by a central production service. *Brevity* and *spontaneity* are the basis for the guidelines. While a production's use of a copyrighted work might meet the brevity requirement, it probably will not meet that of spontaneity. According to the Senate, **spontaneity** is when a teacher acts on his or her own as opposed to copying "done by the educational institution, school system, or larger unit or where copying was required or suggested by the school administration." [4]

Furthermore, in its discussion of Section 107's four factors, the Senate indicated that "amount and substantiality used" referred to extracts but "should not be construed as permitting a *teacher* [emphasis added] to make multiple copies of the same work on a repetitive basis or for *continued use* [emphasis added]." [5] And under "effect of the use upon the potential market," the Senate maintained:

> Fair use is essentially supplementary by nature, and classroom copying that exceeds the legitimate teaching aims such as filling in missing information or bringing a subject up to date would go beyond the proper bounds of fair use. Isolated instances of minor infringements, when multiplied many times, become in the aggregate a major inroad on copyright that must be prevented. [6]

Thus, neither the guidelines nor the four fair use criteria appear to apply to productions—whether produced by nonprofit educational institutions or commercial firms.

However, if the fair use guidelines do not apply to media productions, the basic concept of fair use has some application. For example, Congress noted that while

> the availability of the fair use doctrine to educational broadcasters would be narrowly circumscribed in the case of motion pictures and other audiovisual works . . . under appropriate circumstances it could apply to the nonsequential showing of an individual still or slide, or to the performance of a short excerpt from a motion picture for criticism or comment. [7]

The fine line between a work's proper use in criticism and its exploitation focuses on whether the expression or idea is used. If a work's expression is examined, you have more latitude for using excerpts because you are involved in criticism's true function: the analysis of a creator's abilities. But if the subject of your criticism is the same as the work, you have less latitude because the danger of using the work for its original purpose and intrinsic value is greater. So a criticism of a film of a Shakespearean play using film clips would have a greater claim to fair use than a film on Shakespeare using film clips of the same filmed version. The latter film would be an exploitation of the filmmaker's work for its own purposes. [8]

FAIR USE AND THE JUDICIARY

Since "the line which must be drawn between fair use and copyright infringement depends on an examination of the facts in each case," [9] here is a sampling of how the courts have ruled on fair use and production-related issues:

American Geophysical Union v. Texaco, Inc.. Scientific and technical journal publishers accused Texaco of large-scale, unauthorized copying and making only token payments to the

Copyright Clearance Center (CCC). The publishers wanted maximum damages and a permanent injunction barring Texaco from copying CCC works unless authorized or until Texaco begins making accurate payments. The case is still in court. [10]

Berlin v. E. C. Publications. The plaintiffs, who owned the copyrights to numerous popular songs, claimed the defendants' magazaine, *Mad*, had infringed twenty-five of their songs in an issue which ran a collection of fifty-seven parodies of old standard songs. The parodies indicated which aspect of modern life was being satirized and what tune to sing the parody to, but no music was included. The courts held this was a fair use. [11]

Broadway Music v. F-R Publishing. The plaintiff owned the copyright for the 1914 song "Poor Pauline"; the defendant published a weekly magazine, *The New Yorker*. The plaintiff claimed that the defendant's use of fragments of the song's lyrics in an obituary on Pearl White, the actress who portrayed Pauline in the *Perils of Pauline*, was an infringement of copyright. The court disagreed. It saw no impact on the value of the song and the complaint was dismissed. [12]

Bruzzone v. Miller Brewing Co.. Bruzzone used five to six frames of Miller's copyrighted TV commercials in marketing research. The court held that Bruzzone's use was within the scope of fair use. [13]

College Entrance Book Company v. Amsco Book Company. Both companies published "cram" books. In this case, College Entrace charged Amsco with infringing two of its copyrighted books by using the word lists, English translation, and French articles. Otherwise the books were different. The Second Circuit reversed the district court's dismissal because both books "met exactly the same demand on the same market, and defendant's copying was unquestionably to avoid the trouble or expense of independent work. This is unfair use." [14]

Henry Holt and Company v. Liggett and Myers Tobacco. The defendant's widely distributed pamphlet *Some Facts About Cigarettes* included some quotations from *The Human Voice, Its Care and*

Development, a scientific work written and published by the plaintiffs. The plaintiffs averred that the use of these quotations in a commercial pamphlet reflected poorly on the author's professional ethics and hurt the book's sales. The defendant claimed that the pamphlet only copied a negligible quantity of the scientific work and thus was within the limits of fair use. Furthermore, the author of the scientific work had been acknowledged.

The court upheld a long-standing view of copyright infringement:

> In order to constitute an infringement of the copyright of a book it is not necessary that the whole or even a large portion of the book shall have been copied. It is sufficient if a material and substantial part shall have been copied even though it be but a small part of the work. [15]

The court also maintained that acknowledging the source "does not excuse the infringement." [16] The court, therefore, refused the defendant's motion to dismiss the bill of complaint.

Miller Brewing Company v. Carling O'Keefe Breweries of Canada. Carling's Highlite beer was similar in name and advertisements to Miller's High Life, Lite, and Lowenbrau. The court, in granting Miller's motion for a preliminary injunction, commented: "An infringement of a copyright can be found where only a small portion of a work is copied so long as the part usurped is material and substantial." [17]

Mills Music, Inc. V. State of Arizona. The Ninth Circuit affirmed the district court's judgment for plaintiff. Mills Music claimed that Arizona infringed the copyrighted musical composition "Happiness Is" by its unauthorized use in promoting the 1971 Arizona State Fair. Arizona claimed Eleventh Amendment immunity to prosecution. The circuit court refused to accept this defense: "it is clear that the abrogation of a state's Eleventh Amendment immunity is inherent in the Copyright and Patent Clause and the Copyright Act." [18]

Nichols v. Universal Pictures Corporation. Anne Nichols, the author of the play *Abie's Irish Rose,* alleged that Universal's movie *The Cohens and the Kellys* was taken from her work. The district court dismissed the complaint because "mere ideas are not protected but the manner of expressing the same ideas may be secured and the line differentiating the idea from the expression of the idea is not always clearly defined." [19] Affirming the decision, the Second Circuit stated: "the question is whether the part so taken is 'substantial,' and, therefore, not a 'fair use' of the copyrighted work." [20]

Shapiro, Bernstein & Co. v. P. F. Collier & Son. A story published in *Collier's National Weekly* quoted approximately ten of eighteen lines of the first chorus of the plaintiff's song, "You Can't Stop Me from Lovin' You." Neither the music nor full lyrics were supplied. The court ruled that the song's value had not been impaired, but "if substantial connected portions of the song had been taken, or if the story or incident was adopted as a subterfuge for presenting the song to the public, it would be quite different." [21] The complaint was dismissed.

Wainwright Securities Inc. v. Wall Street Transcript Corporation. Wainwright Securities obtained an injunction preventing the *Wall Street Transcript* (a weekly newspaper) from publishing abstracts of Wainwright's in-depth business analyses. In answer to the newspaper's arguments of fair use and First Amendment coverage for news reporting, the court reverted to the idea-expression dichotomy: "the essence or purpose of legitimate journalism is the reporting of objective facts of developments, not the appropriation of the form of expression used by the news service." [22]

Walt Disney Productions v. Air Pirates. Disney claimed Air Pirates infringed copyrighted cartoon characters by their un-authorized use in adult counter-culture comic books. Air Pirates countered by claiming their use of the characters was a parody—that is, a fair use. The Ninth Circuit affirmed the district court's finding of copyright infringement: "While other factors in the fair use calculus may not be sufficient by themselves to preclude the fair use defense, this and other courts have accepted the traditional American rule that excessive copying precludes fair use." [23]

Though fair use lacks a specific definition, as you can see from the few cases summarized here, the courts look askance at substantial copying, especially when the copy affects the original's marketplace value. Also, acknowledging the source and "second-hand" news reporting do not count as fair use. On a more positive note, fair use does apply in some for-profit situations.

Some other factors the courts might consider in determining fair use include:

● degree of exposure: A single use before a small audience rather than multiple use before a large public audience;

● level of premeditation: A spontaneous use rather than a systematic, continuing use; and,

● honesty of use: The use is made in good faith with no attempt at deception or dishonesty. [24]

REFERENCES

1. Section 107.
2. *Senate*, p. 62; *House*, p. 66.
3. See Sinofsky, pp. 121-125, for a list of producers who do/don't accept fair use guidelines.
4. *Senate*, p. 63.
5. *Senate*, p. 65.
6. *Senate*, p. 65.
7. *Senate*, p. 65; *House*, pp. 72-73.
8. For a discussion of this problem, see Brian S. O'Malley, "Fair Use and Audiovisual Criticism," *COMM/ENT* 4 (Spring 1982): 419-443.
9. *Meeropol v. Nizer*, 195 U.S.P.Q. 273, 278 (2d Cir. 1977).
10. *PTCJ* 30 (9 May 1985): 32; *PTCJ* 32 (26 June 1985): 197-198.
11. 219 F. Supp. 911, 138 U.S.P.Q. 298 (S.D.N.Y. 1963), *aff'd*, 329 F.2d 541, 141 U.S.P.Q. 1 (2d Cir. 1964), *cert. denied*, 379 U.S. 822, 143 U.S.P.Q. 464 (1964).
12. 31 F. Supp. 817, 45 U.S.P.Q. 309 (S.D.N.Y. 1940).
13. 202 U.S.P.Q. 809 (N.D. Cal. 1979).
14. 49 U.S.P.Q. 517, 519 (2d Cir. 1941).
15. 37 U.S.P.Q. 449, 450-451 (E.D. Pa. 1938).
16. 37 U.S.P.Q. 449, 451 (E.D. Pa. 1938).
17. 199 U.S.P.Q. 470, 480 (W.D.N.Y. 1978).
18. 201 U.S.P.Q. 437, 442 (9th Cir. 1979).
19. 2 U.S.P.Q. 139, 142 (S.D.N.Y. 1929).
20. 7 U.S.P.Q. 84, 86 (2d Cir. 1930).
21. 20 Copy. Dec. 656, 659 (S.D.N.Y. 1934).
22. 194 U.S.P.Q. 401, 404 (2d Cir. 1977).
23. 199 U.S.P.Q. 769, 776 (9th Cir. 1978).
24. Ernest T. Sanchez, *Copyright and You* (Washington, DC: National Federation of Local Cable Programmers, n.d.), p. 6.

CHAPTER 6:

PERFORMANCE AND DISPLAY EXEMPTIONS

Just as Section 107 allows certain unauthorized duplications of copyrighted works, Section 110 authorizes certain performances and displays of copyrighted materials. Unlike Section 107, Section 110 does not restrict the amount of a work you may perform or display, but it imposes other restrictions.

CLASSROOM PERFORMANCES AND DISPLAYS

Section 110. Limitations on exclusive rights: Exemption of certain performances and displays

Notwithstanding the provisions of section 106, the following are not infringements of copyright:
(1) performance or display of a work by instructors or pupils in the course of face-to-face teaching activities of a nonprofit educational institution, in a classroom or similar place devoted to instruction, unless, in the case of a motion picture or other audiovisual work, the performance, or the display of individual images, is given by means of a copy that was not lawfully made under this title, and that the person responsible for the performance knew or had reason to believe was not lawfully made; [1]

This section sets forth the performance and display exemption requirements for "face-to-face teaching activities." It excludes recreational or entertainment performances/displays (see also the discussion of public performance in Chapter 4) and illegal copies of audiovisual works. [2]

The phrase **instructors or pupils** "rul[es] out performances by actors, singers, or instrumentalists brought in from outside the school to put on a program" but is "broad enough to include guest lecturers if their instructional activities remain confined to [a] classroom situation." [3] **Nonprofit educational institutions** excludes such for-profit institutions as dance studios and language schools. The **classroom or similar place** restriction means, for example, that "performances in an auditorium or stadium during a school assembly, graduation ceremony, class play, or sporting event, where the audience is not confined to the members of a particular class, would fall outside the scope of clause (1)," [4] but some cases may be exempt under clause (4). A library or gym used as a classroom for systematic instruction would qualify as a "similar place." [5]

INSTRUCTIONAL BROADCASTS OF NONDRAMATIC WORKS

Section 110.   Limitations on exclusive rights: Exemption of certain performances and displays

Notwithstanding the provisions of section 106, the following are not infringements of copyright: . . . .
(2) performance of a nondramatic literary or musical work or display of a work, by or in the course of a transmission, if—

> (A) the performance or display is a regular part of the systematic instructional activities of a governmental body or a nonprofit educational institution; and
> (B) the performance or display is directly related and of material assistance to the teaching content of the transmission; and

(C) the transmission is made primarily for—
(i) reception in classrooms or similar places normally devoted to instruction, or
(ii) reception by persons to whom the transmission is directed because their disabilities or other special circumstances prevent their attendance in classrooms or similar places normally devoted to instruction, or
(iii) reception by officers or employees of governmental bodies as a part of their official duties or employment; [6]

This section deals with instructional broadcasting, that is, broadcasts that are adjuncts to actual classroom instruction as opposed to cultural or educational public broadcasts. Three conditions must be met as listed in subsections A-C. Also, this exempts only performances of nondramatic literary or musical works. Nondramatic literary or musical works exclude operas, musical comedies, motion pictures, and other audiovisual works. Broadcast or transmission of these works requires a license. In-house transmission licenses for educational films and videos are often available free of charge or for a modest cost. In-house transmission licenses for other items may be more difficult to obtain.

PERFORMANCE DURING RELIGIOUS SERVICES

Section 110. Limitations on exclusive rights: Exemption of certain performances and displays

Notwithstanding the provisions of section 106, the following are not infringements of copyright: . . . .
(3) performance of a nondramatic literary or musical work or of a dramatico-musical work of a religious nature, or display of a work, in the course of services at a place of worship or other religious assembly; [7]

To be exempt under this section, the performance or display must be "in the course of services." This "excludes activities at a place of worship that are for social, educational, fund raising, or entertainment purposes" and "would not extend to religious broadcasts or other transmissions to the public at large, even where the transmissions were sent from the place of worship" [8] unless properly licensed. The law quoted above also excludes showing of motion pictures and other audiovisual works in religious services. However, films distributed in "church markets" frequently include the right to perform them in religious settings. [9]

Unlike subsection (2), this subsection includes dramatico-musical works of a religious nature. As the House noted:

> The purpose here is to exempt certain performances of sacred music that might be regarded as "dramatic" in nature, such as oratorios, contatas, musical settings of the mass, choral services, and the like. The exemption is not intended to cover performances of secular operas, musical plays, motion pictures, and the like, even if they have an underlying religious or philosophical theme and take place "in the course of [religious] services." [10]

The House's specific exclusion of secular operas and the like probably stemmed from the spate of court cases generated by unauthorized performances of "Jesus Christ Superstar." [11]

BENEFIT PERFORMANCES

Section 110. Limitations on exclusive rights: Exemption of certain performances and displays

Notwithstanding the provisions of section 106, the following are not infringements of copyright: . . . .

(4) performance of a nondramatic literary or musical work otherwise than in a transmission to the public, without any purpose of direct or indirect commercial advantage and without payment of any fee or other compensation for the performance to any of its performers, promoters, or organizers, if—

(A) there is no direct or indirect admission charge; or
(B) the proceeds, after deducting the reasonable costs of producing the performance, are used exclusively for educational, religious, or charitable purposes and not the private financial gain, except where the copyright owner has served notice of objection to the performance under the following conditions;

(i) the notice shall be in writing and signed by the copyright owner or such owner's duly authorized agent; and
(ii) the notice shall be served on the person responsible for the performance at least seven days before the date of the performance, and shall state the reasons for the objection; and
(iii) the notice shall comply, in form, content, and manner of service, with requirements that the Register of Copyrights shall prescribe by regulation; [12]

Once again, audiovisual works and dramatico-musical works such as operas are excluded from the exemption. Subsection (B) allows the copyright owner to decide whether and under what conditions the work may be performed. "Otherwise, owners could be compelled to make involuntary donations to the fund-raising activities of causes to which they are opposed." [13]

If you carefully read this subsection, you will notice that there is no mention of HOW a copyright owner will learn of the proposed performance. But, should copyright owners object to Section 110(4) uses of their material, the Copyright Office has a procedure for serving a "Notice of Objection." There is no printed form. The letter must clearly state that the copyright owner objects to the performance, refer to Section 110(4) (or description of this section's provision), give the date and place of the performance to which the objection is being made; identify the particular nondramatic literary or musical work(s) whose performance is being objected to; state the reason for the objection; and include the signature of each copyright owner (or owner's duly authorized agent). [14]

PUBLIC RECEPTION OF TRANSMISSIONS

Section 110. Limitations on exclusive rights: Exemption of certain performances and displays

Notwithstanding the provisions of section 106, the following are not infringements of copyright: . . . .
(5) communication of a transmission embodying a performance or display of a work by the public reception of the transmission on a single receiving apparatus of a kind commonly used in private homes, unless—
(A) a direct charge is made to see or hear the transmission; or
(B) the transmission thus received is further transmitted to the public; [15]

Section 110(5) deals with questions raised in *Buck v. Jewell-LaSalle Realty Co.* and *Twentieth Century Music Corp. v. Aiken.* [16] "It applies to performances and displays of all types of works, and its purpose is to exempt from copyright liability anyone who merely turns on, in a public place, an ordinary radio or television receiving apparatus of a kind commonly sold to members of the public for private use." [17] It does not cover cable television (CATV) or situations where the audience is charged to see or hear the transmission.

For more than forty years the *Jewell-LaSalle* rule was thought to require a business establishment to obtain copyright licenses before it could legally pick up any broadcasts off the air and retransmit them to its guest and patrons. As reinterpreted by the *Aiken* decision, the rule of *Jewell-LaSalle* applies only if the broadcast being retransmitted was itself unlicensed. [18]

But, the definition of **perform** in Section 101 overturned the basis of the *Aiken* decision. So the House committee accepted the pre-*Aiken, Jewell-LaSalle* decision; *Aiken* became the outer limit of Section 110(5).

According to the House, Section 110(5) exempts

small commercial establishments whose proprietors merely bring onto their premises standard radio or television equipment and turn it on for their customers' enjoyment, but it would impose liability where the proprietor has a commercial "sound system" installed or converts a standard home receiving apparatus (by augmenting it with sophisticated or extensive amplification equipment) into the equivalent of a commercial sound system. Factors to consider in particular cases would include the size, physical arrangement, and noise level of the areas within the establishment where the transmissions are made audible or visible, and the extent to which the receiving apparatus is altered or augmented for the purpose of improving the aural or visual quality of the performance for individual members of the public using those areas. [19]

Others cases involving Section 110(5) include *BMI v. U.S. Shoe* and *Sailor Music v. The Gap.* [20]

PERFORMANCE EXEMPTIONS FOR FAIRS, RETAILERS, AND DISABLED PERSONS

Sections 110(6), (7), (8), and (9) are of less interest to educational and industrial media producers and are therefore only briefly summarized here.

Section 110(6): The governmental body or nonprofit organization sponsoring the agricultural or horticultural fair or exhibition is exempt when it involves the nondramatic performance of a musical work. But concessionaires are not covered by this exemption.

Section 110(7): This section covers retailers of phonorecords by allowing them to perform a nondramatic musical work or sound recording when the sole purpose of the performance is to promote sales of the work.

Sections 110(8) and 110(9): These sections exempt certain transmissions to the blind and other disabled persons of nondramatic literary works. [21]

PERFORMANCES AT SOCIAL FUNCTIONS

Section 110. Limitations on exclusive rights: Exemption of certain performances and displays

Notwithstanding the provisions of section 106, the following are not infringements of copyright: . . . .
(10) notwithstanding paragraph 4 above, the following is not an infringement of copyright: performance of a nondramatic literary or musical work in the course of a social function which is organized and promoted by a nonprofit veterans' organization or a nonprofit fraternal organization to which the general public is not invited, but not including the invitees of the organization, if the proceeds from the performance, after deducting the reasonable costs of producing the performance, are used exclusively for charitable purposes and not for financial gain. For purposes of this section the social functions of any college or university fraternity or sorority shall not be included unless the social function is held solely to raise funds for a specific charitable purpose. [22]

Added by a 1982 amendment, this subsection clarifies Section 110(4). It exempts performances of nondramatic literary and musical works for certain fraternal organizations—even if they were not exempt under Section 110(4).

Nimmer raised two questions about this section: (1) What is meant by "invitees"? (2) Which organizations are exempt? In answer to the first question, Nimmer opined that invitees are probably limited to those receiving personal invitations from an organization's members. The answer to the second question poses more problems since Congressional intent was to exempt organizations whose primary purpose is charitable service to the community. This would seem to exclude financial, social, and political organizations. According to Nimmer, even if an organization does not devote itself exclusively to charitable service, it may still be exempt if all proceeds of the performance (minus costs) go to charitable purposes. Conversely, if an organization's primary purpose is other than charitable, it will not be exempt even if the proceeds go to charity. [23] College and university fraternities and sororities are the one exception. They are exempt if the performance is a fund-raiser for a specific charitable purpose.

REFERENCES

1. Section 110(1).
2. *Senate*, p. 73; *House*, p. 81.
3. *Senate*, p. 74; *House*, p. 82.
4. *Senate*, p. 74; *House*, p. 82.
5. For an in-depth treatment of this section, see Jerome K. Miller, *Using Copyrighted Videocassettes in Classrooms and Libraries* (Friday Harbor, WA: Copyright Information Services, 1984).
6. Section 110(2).
7. Section 110(3).
8. *Senate*, p. 76; *House*, p. 84.
9. For an in-depth treatment of this topic, see Jerome K. Miller, *Video Copyright Guidelines for Pastors & Church Workers* (New York: National Council of the Churches of Christ, 1986).
10. *House*, p. 84.
11. For example, *Robert Stigwood Group v. O'Reilly*, 457 F.2d 50 (2d Cir. 1972).
12. Section 110(4).
13. *House*, p. 86.
14. For a full description of the procedure, see 37 C.F.R. §201.13 (1986).
15. Section 110(5).
16. *Jewell-LaSalle*, 283 U.S. 191 (1931); *Aiken*, 422 U.S. 151 (1975).
17. *House*, p. 86.
18. *House*, pp. 86-87.
19. *House*, p. 87.
20. *BMI*, 217 U.S.P.Q. 224 (9th Cir. 1982); *Sailor Music*, 688 F.2d 84 (2d Cir. 1981).
21. Sections 110(6)-(9).
22. 17 U.S.C.A. §110(10).
23. *Nimmer on Copyright* (New York: Matthew Bender, 1984, 1986): §8.15[H].

CHAPTER   7:

DURATION   OF   COPYRIGHT

As a producer, you need to know how long a copyright lasts, for two reasons.   One, you want to benefit from your copyrighted work for as long as possible.   Two, since public domain works provide low-cost production resources, knowing when a work enters the public domain can make a difference in your budget and permissions requests.

Chapter 3 of the Copyright Act deals with duration.   Due to the somewhat lengthy nature of the various sections, they are summarized but not reproduced here (see Appendix D11 for the Copyright Office summary in Circular R22). [1]

For the purposes of duration, there are two major categories of works: (1) those created on or after January 1, 1978, and (2) those copyrighted before 1978.   (The 1976 Copyright Act took effect January 1, 1978.)

WORKS CREATED ON OR AFTER JANUARY 1, 1978

Works in this category include those actually created on or after January 1, 1978, and those in existence but not published, registered, or in the public domain on January 1, 1978.

The basic copyright term is life of the author plus fifty years. In the case of a joint work (i.e., two or more authors) not made for hire, the term is the life of the last surviving author plus fifty years after that author's death. If the work is made for hire (for example, produced and copyrighted by a corportion), anonymous, or pseudonymous, the term is seventy-five years from its first publication OR one hundred years from its creation—whichever is shorter. (If at least one author of an anonymous or pseudonymous work is identified, the life plus fifty years term applies.)

These terms also apply to works created before January 1, 1978, but not registered or in the public domain. Congress added special protection for these works by guaranteeing copyright in them at least until December 31, 2002. And, if published before then, until December 31, 2027.

WORKS ALREADY COPYRIGHTED

This category includes works either in their first twenty-eight-year copyright term or in their renewal term. (Under the 1909 Copyright Act, a copyright lasted twenty-eight years and could be renewed for an additonal twenty-eight years.)

If the copyright in a work in its first twenty-eight-year term is renewed at the proper time, the second term will last forty-seven years for a total duration of seventy-five years. If the copyright is not renewed, the work enters the public domain. For example, a work copyrighted in 1970 is eligible for renewal in 1998. If the copyright is renewed, the work will be protected until 2045. Otherwise, the work enters the public domain on January 1, 1999.

The 1976 Act automatically extended the renewal term for works already in their second copyright term to forty-seven years for a total of seventy-five years. In other words, their copyrights expire at the end of the year seventy-five years from the date of their original copyright. Thus a work copyrighted in 1945 and renewed in 1973 is protected until January 1, 2021.

REFERENCES

1. Sections 301-305.

CHAPTER   8:

NOTICE,   DEPOSIT,   AND   REGISTRATION

Chapter 4 of the 1976 Act deals with copyright notice, deposit, and registration.   Portions are summarized here. [1]

NOTICE OF COPYRIGHT

Sections 401 and 402 set forth the basic requirements for "visually perceptible copies" (perceptible with or without the aid of a machine) and "phonorecords of sound recordings":

(A) The notice is required whenever a work is published—regardless of where or when it was first published.

(B) The notice consists of three elements:

- the symbol © or the word **Copyright** or the abbreviation **Copr**; the symbol ℗ for phonorecords;

- the year of first publication; and,

- the copyright owner's name.

(C) The notice must be affixed to the copies in a way that gives reasonable notice of the copyright claim.

The notice you usually see runs:

Copyright © Year Full Name
All rights reserved.

This format is favored by publishers because it covers notice requirements in countries committed to the Universal Copyright Convention (UCC) and the Buenos Aires Convention. These two conventions are the major international agreements governing copyright protection. The requirements for copyright notices are summarize in Copyright Office Circular R96 which is reproduced in Appendix D4.

DEPOSIT FOR THE LIBRARY OF CONGRESS

Section 407 mandates that all works published in the U.S. with a copyright notice be deposited with the Library of Congress. This mandatory deposit ensures that the Library of Congress receives copies of every copyrighted work published in the U.S.

Section 407's basic requirement: Within ninety days after a work has been published with notice of copyright in the U.S., the copyright owner must deposit two complete copies or two complete phonorecords of the best edition in the Copyright Office. Circular R40b, reproduced in Appendix D5, describes the deposit requirements for visual arts materials.

If copies are not deposited, the Register of Copyrights may demand in writing the required deposit. Failure to comply with the written demand can result in a fine of not more than $250 per work plus the retail price of the copies. Repeated or willful refusal to comply may result in an added fine of $2500. The Library of Congress seeks out non-complying publications and, with the assistance of the Justic Department, enforces this mandatory deposit requirement.

REGISTRATION

The 1909 Act treated depositing copies of a work for the Library of Congress collection and for copyright registration as the same thing. The 1976 Act regards deposit and registration as separate though related requirements. Generally, you must deposit copies of your work with the Library of Congress. Copyright registration per se is not required. Your work automatically receives copyright protection at the time it is created, that is, "fixed" in a copy or phonorecord for the first time. However, there are advantages to registering your work:

- You establish a public record of your copyright claim.

- You must register your work before you can bring an infringement suit.

- You have more remedies against infringement if you register your work on time. If an infringement occurs before registration, a copyright owner is entitled to the ordinary remedies of injunction and actual damages. If the infringement occurs after registration, the copyright owner may be entitled to attorney's fees and statutory damages.

Prompt registration also provides remedies for the inadvertent omission of copyright notices.

To use your deposit copies for copyright registration be sure the appropriate application and fee accompany the deposit. If sent separately, the deposit copies will be used for the Library of Congress but not for registration. The basic application and supplemental forms are listed in Appendix D6.

Deciding which form to use can be tricky. For example, Circular R56, *Copyright for Sound Recordings*, notes that "sounds accompanying a motion picture or other audiovisual work should *not* [emphasis in original] be registered on Form SR" because the Copyright Act does not define these sounds as sound recordings. These sounds are an integral part of the motion picture or audiovisual work which are classified as works of the performing arts. They should be registered on Form PA. [2]

The circular also states that "a musical composition is classified as a work of the performing arts." Therefore, "to register only the musical composition (not the particular sounds or recorded performance) you should use Form PA, even though your deposit may be a phonorecord."[3]   In other words, the medium in which it is fixed does not affect the composition's classification as a work of the performing arts.

Multimedia kits are another area highlighted by R56:

Form SR is the appropriate form for registration of a multimedia kit which combines two or more kinds of authorship including a sound recording (such as kit containing a book and an audiocassette).

If, however, the work contains a visual element which requires the use of a machine for projection (such as slides or a filmstrip), the work is considered an audiovisual work and should be registered on Form PA. [4]

The chart reproduced in Appendix D7 provides further assistance in determining when to use Forms PA and SR.

REFERENCES

1. Sections 401-402, 407, 411, and 412; see also Edward R. Hearn, "Legal Aspects of Video Production," *Video Systems* (August 1987): 48; 52.
2. (Washington, DC: Government Printing Office, 1985): p. 3.
3. Circular R56, p. 3.
4. Circular R56, p. 3.

PART II

SELECTED PRODUCTION ISSUES

CHAPTER 9:

BASIC PROCEDURES

Producing materials, whether for educational, industrial, or commercial usage, entails more than knowing the design process. **Producing** also means making sure you indeed have the legal right to use the various elements (e.g., script, music, photographs) of your production. A copyright infringement suit against a school district often includes the actual infringer, the contributory infringers, plus the district superintendent and the school board. In industry, corporate officers and principal stockholders may be held personally liable for any infringement. Imagine how popular you will be with a quarter-of-a-million dollar lawsuit facing your college, school district, or corporation!

As noted in the "Preface," this book is a primer and, as such, does not cover every facet of a producer's responsibilities. It focuses on a selection of key areas that can cause legal headaches for the producer. Figure 9.1 lists most of these areas. You might want to compile a similar checklist, including items important to your situation, for your production-forms folder. [1]

Identifying basic procedures is hard because of the unique requirements of each production. At best, there two procedures common to all productions; a third covers many production situations.

Figure 9.1 Sinofsky's By No Means
Exhaustive Checklist of Items Requiring
Clearance Before Use in a Production

Production Title: _____

Item	Date Requested	Date Granted	Conditions

Underlying Rights

Literary Property Rights

Adaption, Remake, Other Rights

Character/Sequel Rights

Title

Identifiable Names/Places/Products

Visuals

Talent (releases/union contracts)

Performance Rights

Music

Reprint Rights

Public Domain Status Investigated

PROCEDURE #1:

CONSULT LEGAL COUNSEL
BEFORE YOU START YOUR PRODUCTION.

This may strike you as an unusual place to begin. Some may even consider it oversimplistic or an insult to their intelligence. Do not be insulted and do not discount the value of good legal advice. Productions can be complex. You are expected to be familiar with laws such as copyright, privacy, trademark, and unfair competition while juggling union contracts. Contracts—the plural—because you may be working with several unions at once; for example, the Writers Guild of America, the Screen Actors Guild (SAG), and the American Federation of Musicians (AFM). Even a "simple" in-house, educational production may require a form or two.

The best time to obtain your legal advice is BEFORE any damage is done. This saves time and energy and prevents missed deadlines. You will have the music, photographs, and other resources you want when you need them.

PROCEDURE #2:

NEGOTIATE, NEGOTIATE, NEGOTIATE!

Another reason to consult your lawyer is for help in developing releases (discussed in Chapter 12) and negotiating contracts. There is no such thing as a "standard" production contract per se. Selz and Simensky list several reasons for changing the forms they show in their book:

- Forms identify areas to be discussed in a particular deal.

- Law and business practices change.

- The authors would not use some of the forms as written though others would.

- Forms are not a negotiated agreement.

- Since agreements can reflect either side's point of view, there are at least two ways to draft a contract.

- Some forms are copyrighted. [That is, you would need permission to duplicate them.] [2]

Since each contract reflects the needs of its particular production, someone must negotiate anew each agreement. Whom better than your lawyer to help you bargain? (See Appendix B3 for selected sources of sample forms.)

PROCEDURE #3:

REQUEST PERMISSION—IN WRITING.

Some production needs can be handled by simply writing to the copyright owner for permission to use the work. But do not wait until the last moment to write because it may take several weeks to process your request. If, due to time constraints, you telephone first, follow up with a letter stating the specific terms agreed upon.

Seek permission for the specific item and specific use you want to make of it. Your chances of receiving permission for a specific instance are greater than for a blanket request. Asking for blanket permission may involve you in formal licensing agreements.

The more complete the information you supply in your request, the quicker the copyright owner's response. Your data should include an accurate rendering of the author, title, edition, year of copyright, what will be used (e.g., the amount; page/line/frame number), when and with whom will it be used, how many copies will be made and in what medium, how and where will the copies be distributed, and whether the copies will be sold. Be sure to include a complete return address and possibly a self-addressed envelope.

Once you obtain the desired permission, be sure to comply with all the terms set forth by the copyright owner.

Producers addresses are listed in sources such as the *Literary Market Place, Ulrich's International Periodicals, Audio Visual Market Place, American Art Directory, Kemps International Film and Television Yearbook,* and *Kemps International Music and Recording Industry Yearbook* (additional sources are listed with their respective topics).

These then are the basic procedures for producers to follow. The remaining chapters discuss specific areas of concern to producers.

REFERENCES

1. For other production checklists see, for example, Barry Hampe, "Budgeting a Production Part I," *Technical Photography* 18 (December 1986): 44-47 and "Budgeting a Production Part II," *Technical Photography* 19 (March 1987): 16; 21; 45; and Edward R. Hearn, "Legal Aspects of Video Production," *Video Systems* (August 1987): 52; 54; 58.
2. *Entertainment Law: Legal Concepts and Business Practices*, 3 vols. (Colorado Springs, CO: Shepard's/McGraw-Hill, 1984), 3:F-5.

CHAPTER   10:

SCRIPTS,   TITLES,   CHARACTERS,   ETC.

As the producer, it is your responsibility to obtain clear rights to the literary property (i.e., script); the production's title; fictional characters; and identifiable names, products, and locations.

SCRIPTS

According to Farber, nine methods exist for acquiring rights to the literary property desired:

1.   use materials in the public domain;

2.   commission an adaptation of a public domain work;

3.   commission a translation of a public domain work;

4.   acquire the rights to an adaptation or translation of a public domain work (the adaptation or translation may be protected though the underlying work is in the public domain);

5.   acquire the rights to an original copyrighted work;

6.   acquire the rights to an adaptation or translation of an original copyrighted work;

7.   acquire the right to adapt or translate an original copyrighted work;

8. commission an original work you then copyright; or,

9. write your own work. [1]

The key question: Who owns the rights to this literary property? As discussed in Part I, if the script is entirely your own creation, that is, you (or an employee working for hire) created, developed, and wrote the script, then you (or the organization who hired you or the employee) own the copyright. But, if your script is a derivative work, that is, there are underlying rights such as a copyrighted work or protected character involved, you must investigate the ownership of these rights and obtain the proper clearances.

There are three possible investigators: yourself; the Copyright Office; or, a recognized copyright specialist. The general procedures involved in the first two types of investigations are outlined in an excerpt from Copyright Office Circular R22 reproduced in Appendix D8. Circular R1b, reproduced in Appendix D9, lists some of the disadvantages of a Copyright Office search. These same limitations can apply to a do-it-yourself search.

The Washington, D.C. firm of Brylawski, Cleary & Leeds (see Appendix A for address) best exemplifies the third type of investigator. While the firm does not actually clear titles or secure copyright permissions, it does advise and counsel on matters relating to securing such clearances. The firm searches the Copyright Office's records, Library of Congress resources, and its own library of various bibliographic sources including an extensive file card index of entertainment industry trade clippings. Other searchers and their areas of specialization are identified in Jerome K. Miller's *The Copyright Directory, Vol. 1: General Information*, Chapter 3. Figure 10.1 reproduces a sample Brylawski, Cleary & Leeds copyright search.

Once you identify the owner of the literary property rights, you then negotiate for those rights you need. These might include worldwide exclusivity, home videos, sequels, characters, foreign language versions, and adaptations of the basic work. You should

Figure 10.1 Sample Copyright Search
(Reproduced here with the kind permission of Brylawski, Cleary & Leeds)

Replying to your recent request, I find that the popular television series entitled FAMILY originally appeared on the ABC-TV network as a mini-series in six parts beginning March 9, 1976. The series was produced by Spelling-Goldberg Productions in association with Mike Nichols, with each episode fifty-two minutes in length. The series was reportedly created by Jay Presson Allen.

However, I do not find from my search of the Copyright Office a record of registration of a claim of copyright in any of the episodes of the series. Likewise, no assignment of copyright with respect to the series, nor any other document affecting the right, title or interest therein, has been recorded in the Copyright Office.

A novelization of the series entitled FAMILY, as created by Jay Presson Allen and adapted by Leila Andrews, was published by Random House, and copyrighted in the name of Spelling-Goldberg Productions as of a publication date of September 11, 1976 and registered under Entry No. A:793822. This book was also published in paperback by Ballantine in 1976. Two subsequent novelizations, entitled FAMILY, NO. 2 and FAMILY, NO. 3, as adapted by Leila Andrews, were also published in paperback by Ballantine in 1977, but have not as yet been registered.

According to the Hollywood Reporter for March 10, 1977, ABC-TV, Spelling-Goldberg Productions, Ballantine Books and various individuals had been sued by Jeri Emmett Laird, using the pen name J. Devereaux, claiming that she was the author of the TV series "Family". According to the item, she claimed to have submitted the series idea to ABC and Spelling-Goldberg Productions in September 1973, called "Two. . .Four. . .Six. . .Eight". The item indicated that the plaintiff was asking for $1,000,000 in damages for copyright infringement and unspecified punitive and exemplary damages.

In the absence of a registration of claims of copyright in the episodes of this series, it would seem desirable for you to arrange for screening of prints of pictures of the series to determine what copyright notice, if any, appears thereon.

definitely ask for the rights to reproduce, distribute, and prepare derivative works.

If you reach an agreement, you might consider registering it with the Copyright Office to form a public record. No Copyright Office form exists for registering the agreement. Basically, you send the original or a notarized legible photocopy of the agreement with the appropriate fee. Currently, the fee runs $10 for a document of six pages or less covering one title. Additional pages and titles cost 50 cents each. After recordation, the document is returned with a certificate of record. Complete instructions are reproduced in Appendices E1 and E2. [2]

TITLES

Section 102 and its explication in Circular R34 (see Chapter 3), clearly state that "names, titles, and short phrases or expressions are not subject to copyright protection." So why bother obtaining the rights to a title? Producers usually buy the rights to a work for its title and character names, thus protecting themselves under trademark or unfair competition law.

The federal trademark statute, Section 43(a) of the Lanham Act or 15 USC §§1051-1127, expanded the common law concept of unfair competition to include two types of federal torts: (a) false designation of origin, and, (b) false descriptions and misrepresentations. The statute protects both registered and unregistered trademarks. It covers interstate commerce, not local activity. The Lanham Act settles such entertainment industry disputes as project titles, character names and depictions, and unauthorized use of names and merchandise.

Those invoking the Lanham Act also often invoke its state-related companions: unfair competition and antidilution laws. Using similar or identical titles for similar media projects could be "actionable as unfair competition either if the use of such titles, depending on which state law applies, is inherently unfair, or if the title being simulated has acquired secondary meaning." [3] **Secondary meaning** refers to when a word or phrase becomes almost a trademark for a particular producer, product, or the like. **Antidilution laws** protect against the erosion of a trademark or name's distinctive quality—even if a non-competitor's acts do not cause confusion.

Court cases abound in this area. For example:

Orion Pictures v. Dell Publishing. Orion produced a movie entitled *A Little Romance* loosely based upon *E=MC², Mon Amour.* Dell wanted to use the movie's title as the title for its translation of the book. Orion balked at this because it claimed there were great differences between the book and movie. Orion contended that Dell simply wanted a "free ride" on the movie's publicity. The court held for Orion. [4]

Brandon v. The Regents of the University of California. The plaintiff produced a film entitled *Anything You Want to Be* dealing with sex-role stereotyping. Three times she denied sale of a print to the defendant's Extension Media Center (EMC) for rental purposes. In 1974, EMC began distributing *Anything They Want to Be* for which it helped pay production costs. EMC had also rented the Brandon film and loaned it to the independent producers prior to the production of EMC's film. The court described the title as "a brazen act of outright plagiarism" and found substantial similarities in the films themselves. The court also attributed Brandon's decreased profits directly to EMC's film. The court held for the plaintiff. [5]

Allied Artists Pictures Corp. v. Friedman. Allied Artists distributed a French film, *The Story of O.* The film was based upon *Histoire d'O*, published in the early 1950s with a translation distributed by Grove Press. Friedman used a similar title for his own film, *The Journey of O.* The court found for plaintiff. [6]

Titles can be researched. Figure 10.2 is a sample title search by Brylawski, Cleary & Leeds.

Also, if you have a never-used-before title for a theatrical motion picture, you might consider registering it with the Motion Picture Association of America's Motion Picture Title Directory (see

Figure 10.2 Sample Title Search
(Reproduced here with the kind permission of Brylawski, Cleary & Leeds)

Replying to your recent request, I find from my search of the records of the Copyright Office, the card indices of the Library of Congress, and the records and files of this office that the title FIGHTING BACK has been previously used for:

Autobiographical book by Rocky Bleier with Terry O'Neil, published by Stein & Day, August 8, 1975. Published in paperback by Warner Books, 1976. Revised edition published by Stein & Day, 1980.

Television motion picture in 100 mins. running time, based on the book by Rocky Bleier and Terry O'Neil, produced by MTM Enterprises, 1980; premiered on the ABC-TV network, December 7, 1980.

Photoplay in 61 mins. running time, copyrighted by Twentieth Century-Fox Films Corp., July 7, 1948. Copyright renewed. This picture has been variously telecast.

Educational motion picture in 24 mins. running time, produced by National Educational Television and released by Indiana University Audio-Visual Center, 1974.

Photoplay in two reels, copyrighted by Universal Pictures Corp., February 3, 1922.

Photoplay in five reels, released by Triangle Film Corp., November 1, 1917.

Episode NO. 2 in the serial photoplay "The Silent Avenger", copyrighted by Vitagraph Co., 1920.

Book by Charles E. Alverson (a Black Bat mystery), published by Bobbs-Merrill Co., December 20, 1973.

Book by Ronni Sandroff, published by Alfred A. Knopf, May 31, 1978; in paperback by B.J. Publishing Group, 1979.

Figure 10.2 (continued)

Book by Joie H. McGrail (One Woman's Struggle Against Cancer), published by Harper & Row, February 15, 1978.

Book by Margaret C. Keatinge, subtitled "A Manual for Survival with Cancer", published by Vantage Press, 1980.

Sound recording performed by the Hudson Brothers, copyrighted by The Rocket Record Co. Ltd., October 11, 1973.

Nondramatic literary work by J.P. Coakley, copyrighted by the author as a published work, October 29, 1979.

Several unpublished musical compositions which have been copyrighted under this title.

Reference is also made to the following:

FIGHT BACK/WITH DAVID HOROWITZ: Consumer report series, twenty-six shows, 25 mins. running time each, produced and distributed by Group W Productions; premiered on the NBC-TV network the week of September 13, 1980; currently listed as available for television distribution through Group W Productions.

GUNG FU: FIGHTING BACK: Canadian motion picture in 19 mins. running time, directed by Allan Stein, 1974.

FIGHT BACK: A WOMAN'S GUIDE TO SELF DEFENSE: Book by Emil Farkas and Margaret Leeds, published by Holt, Rinehart & Winston, 1978.

FIGHT BACK; DON'T LET THE GYP ARTISTS GET AWAY WITH IT: Folder copyrighted by BAND aka Bay Area Neighborhood Development, September 19, 1966.

FIGHT BACK, AND DON'T GET RIPPED OFF: Book by David Horowitz, published by Harper & Row, 1979.

Appendix A for address).   This will prevent other producers from using an identical or similar title.

FICTIONAL CHARACTERS

A successful character can be worth millions of dollars in character rights.   Simply think of Spielberg's E.T. or any of Lucas's *Star Wars* creations.   Because of the confusion about the copyrightability of characters, producers carefully negotiate character rights.   And, since sequels use the same characters, these rights too are carefully contracted.

Characters begin life as an idea; ideas are not copyrightable.

A general character type or common character such, for example, as a hardboiled, tough-talking, hard-hitting, romantically inclined private detective would fall into the idea category and the appropriation of such character type . . . alone would not constitute copyright infringement. [7]

Just imagine what would happen to the romance industry if tall, handsome, successful heroes could be copyrighted!

Once characters are fully developed expressions, they may be copyrightable.   Cartoon characters are probably the easiest to protect under copyright (see Circular R44 on copyrighting cartoons reproduced in Appendix D10) since the three key elements that constitute a character are clearly delineated: name, physical appearance, and characterization.   Characterization includes everything from mannerisms, habits, and speech to attire, setting, and milieu.   Non-visual characters have a harder time proving their uniqueness of expression for copyright purposes.

Fictional characters may be protected under the doctrine of unfair competition when the character's name and physical appearance are used to mislead the public "into believing that defendant's characters are sponsored or authorized by, or derived from, plaintiff" or "when such name and appearance have acquired secondary meaning, i.e., are sufficiently known to the public as to indicate their particular source." [8] The essence of the doctrine: It is "inequitable for a defendant to profit by 'palming off' his product as the plaintiff's." [9]

Fisher v. Star Co. is an early case in this area. Harry Fisher began publishing the "Mutt and Jeff" comic strips in 1909. When his contract with Star Company expired, he continued selling the comics to other newspapers. The Star Company, meanwhile, employed artists to draw "Mutt and Jeff"-type comics. Fisher filed suit to enjoin further publication of these comics. But his suit was NOT for copyright infringement because the 1909 Act would not have helped him. Instead he filed suit under the doctrine of unfair competition and won. [10]

According to Turner, "the measure of copyright protection afforded to the creator of a literary character is founded upon two cases" [11]: Judge Learned Hand's opinion in *Nichols v. Universal Pictures Corp.* and the Ninth Circuit's in *Warner Brothers v. Columbia Broadcasting System* (CBS).

In *Nichols v. Universal Pictures Corporation*, Anne Nichols, author of the play *Abie's Irish Rose*, alleged that Universal's movie *The Cohens and the Kellys* was taken from her work. In its opinion, the district court looked at the idea-expression dichotomy: "mere ideas are not protected but the manner of expressing the same ideas may be secured and the line differentiating the idea from the expression of the idea is not always clearly defined." [12] In its affirmation of the lower court's decision, the Second Circuit turned to fair use: "[T]he question is whether the part so taken is 'substantial,' and, therefore, not a 'fair use' of the copyrighted work." [13] Both courts thought the play and movie dissimilar and dismissed the complaint.

Warner Brothers v. CBS is often called the *Sam Spade* case because it focused on the use of the detective Dashiell Hammett introduced in *The Maltese Falcon*. In 1930, Hammett granted certain rights in *The Maltese Falcon* to Warner Brothers. These rights did not include future Sam Spade stories. Hammett then wrote a series for CBS, "The Adventures of Sam Spade," which caused Warner Brothers to sue for infringement and unfair use.

[S]ince the use of characters and character names are nowhere specifically mentioned in the agreements, but that other items, including the title, . . ., and their use are specifically mentioned as being granted, . . . the character rights with the names cannot be held to be within the grants, and that under the doctrine of *ejusdem generis* [of the same kind], general language cannot be held to include them. [14]

Thus the author was free to use the characters and character names in other writings. In reaching its decision, the court also commented on the copyrightability of characters:

It is conceivable that the character really constitutes the story being told, but if the character is only the chessman in the game of telling the story he is not within the area of the protection afforded by the copyright. [15]

Other cases dealing with character rights include:

Warner Brothers v. ABC. Warner Brothers charged that ABC's "American Hero" infringed its *Superman* rights. Warner Brothers lost because the court saw both characters as products of the "superhero" genre. [16]

De Costa v. CBS. In 1967, De Costa sued CBS over the character Paladin, who dressed in black and distributed cards reading "Have Gun Will Travel. Wire Paladin." De Costa created such a character for parades and fairs. He won in the district court, but the First Circuit reversed the decision in favor of CBS. [17]

In 1975, De Costa tried to sue CBS once again; this time under common law trademark infringement. He lost this case too. The courts' general feeling was that De Costa had not developed his character beyond the "gunslinger" genre. [18]

Prouty v. NBC. When NBC tried to produce "Stella Dallas" radio skits, Prouty, the author and owner of the original *Stella Dallas* novel, sued and won. [19] The difference in medium did not allow NBC to use that name.

DC Comics v. Filmation Associates. Filmation Associates created two children's TV cartoon series with characters similar to the plaintiff's Aquaman and Plastic Man comic books. The court found for plaintiff. [20]

A corollary to these cases is that "unless abandoned through lack of compliance with legal requisites, the creator or legal successor may protect the name as applied to and signifying his creative product." [21] For example, the character rights in Sherlock Holmes were never abandoned, so care must be taken. As a recent book review noted:

> Eleven years after Rex Stout's death and Nero Wolfe's "withdrawal from practice," Nero and Archie Goodwin are back in business in their old New York City brownstone, thanks to the efforts of Chicago journalist [Robert] Goldsborough, who obtained from the Stout estate the rights to continue Wolfe's adventures. [22]

Beware! The death of the creator does not place characters in the public domain. You still must negotiate for their use.

NAMES, PRODUCTS, AND LOCATIONS

Names, products, and locations also need permission for use. You might recall the stories about E.T.'s predilection for Reese's pieces. In the original script, E.T. supposedly ate M&Ms, but the company is said to have denied Spielberg its permission to use the product. Currently, Sylvester Stallone is negotiating with four Los Angeles area communities to close part of a freeway during rush hour for a trucking scene. Even if you are shooting in-house, clearing your sites with the appropriate office (usually Public Relations) can prevent such mishaps as arriving simultaneously with another production crew or the painters.

One of the better-known disclaimers states: "All characters in this work are fictitious. Any resemblance to actual persons, living or dead, is purely coincidental." In her "Author's Note" to *Murder Must Advertise*, Dorothy Sayers declared: "If, in the course of this fantasy, I have unintentionally used a name or slogan suggestive of any existing person, firm or commodity, it is by sheer accident, and is not intended to cast the slightest reflection upon any actual commodity, firm or person." [23] These disclaimers are to prevent lawsuits for defamation, invasion of privacy, and the like.

Using the names of famous people treads the fine line between informational and commercial benefits. If the use is judged commercial, this may infringe the person's publicity or privacy rights. Chapter 12 discusses this issue in more detail.

REFERENCES

1. Donald C. Farber, *Producing Theatre: A Comprehensive Legal and Business Guide* (New York: Drama Book Publishers, 1981), pp. 8-15.
2. 37 C.F.R. §§201.4, 201.9 (1986); see also the discussion of tranfers in William S. Strong, *The Copyright Book: A Practical Guide*, 2nd ed. (Cambridge, MA: The MIT Press, 1984), Chapter 3.
3. Selz and Simensky, §17.07; see also the discussion in Peter Shapiro, "The Validity of Registered Trademarks for Titles and Characters After the Expiration of Copyright in the Underlying Work," in *ASCAP Copyright Law Symposium* (New York: Columbia University Press, 1984), pp. 79-87.
4. 471 F. Supp. 392 (S.D.N.Y. 1979).
5. 441 F. Supp. 1086 (D.Mass. 1977).
6. 68 Cal. App. 3d 127 (1977).
7. Leonard Zissu, "Whither Character Rights: Some Observations," *Journal of the Copyright Society of the U.S.A.* 28 (1981): 129.
8. Selz and Simensky, §17.27; see also the discussion in Shapiro, pp. 87-101.
9. James L. Turner, "It's a Bird, It's a Plane Or Is It Public Domain?: Analysis of Copyright Protection Afforded Fictional Characters," *South Texas Law Journal* 22 (1982): 344.
10. 231 N.Y. 414 (1921).
11. Turner, p. 345.
12. 2 U.S.P.Q. 142 (S.D.N.Y. 1929).
13. 7 U.S.P.Q. 84, 86 (2d Cir. 1930).
14. 216 F.2d 945, 949 (9th Cir. 1954).
15. 216 F.2d 945, 950 (9th Cir. 1954).
16. 654 F.2d 205 (2d Cir. 1981).
17. 377 F.2d 315 (1st Cir. 1967).
18. 520 F.2d 499 (1st Cir. 1975).
19. 26 F. Supp. 265 (D.Mass. 1939).
20. 486 F. Supp. 1273 (S.D.N.Y. 1980); see also *Walt Disney Production v. Air Pirates* discussed in Chapter 5.
21. Zissu, p. 130.
22. *"Murder in E. Minor"* (Book review), *Booklist* 82 (1 March 1986): 947.
23. (New York: Avon, 1933 [1967 printing]).

CHAPTER 11:

DRAMATIC WORKS

Before turning to production issues such as visuals and music, one type of literary property needs further clarification: drama. The distinction between a dramatic and a nondramatic work is important in applying copyright law. For example, the Section 110 exemption of certain performances seems to allow greater leeway for nondramatic performances than dramatic ones.

DEFINITION

Congress failed to include a definition for dramatic works in Section 101 because the term has a "fairly settled" meaning. [1] As with fair use, legal commentators and the courts have filled this gap.

How can you tell if a work is a drama? A dramatic work can be performed or staged. It tells a story. And, it arouses the emotions (drama's purpose is to stimulate the emotions); but, the courts usually reject this last criterion. [2] According to Nimmer:

> Fundamentally there seem to be but two essential elements for a dramatic composition: (1) that it relate a story, and (2) that it provide directions whereby a substantial portion of the story may be visually or audibly represented to an audience as actually occurring, rather than merely being narrated or described. [3]

In copyright terms, a motion picture is not synonymous with drama or a dramatic work. For example, "a mere exhibition, spectacle or arrangement of scenic effects will not constitute a dramatic work"; nor will "mere ballroom and social dances." [4]

Works in this genre are categorized as dramatic or dramatico-musical (though Nimmer claimed the latter term has generally dropped from usage [5]). A **dramatic work** is a composition which tells a story. "It may be just the narrative or representation of a single occurrence; but it must repeat or mimic some action, speech, emotion, passion, or character, real or imaginary." [6]

A **dramatico-musical composition** contains musical or vocal accompaniment in addition to plot, character, and acting; for example, operas, operettas, and musical comedies. As defined in *Green v. Luby*, a dramatico-musical composition is "a sketch, consisting of a series of recitations and songs, with a very little dialogue and action, and with scenery, and lights thrown upon the singer." [7]

DRAMATICO-MUSICAL V. MUSICAL COMPOSITION

The distinction between a dramatico-musical work and a musical composition is crucial for producers because it affects the scope of the copyright owner's exclusive performance rights. The copyright owner of a dramatico-musical work retains sole public performance rights. But, the public performance rights of a musical composition's copyright owner are limited by Section 110 (discussed in Chapter 6), Section 115 (compulsory license for making phonorecords), Section 116 (juke box compulsory license), and Section 118 (public broadcasting compulsory license).

What constitutes a dramatic performance of a musical composition? "Assuming there is a dramatico-musical composition, what is a dramatic performance and what is a non-dramatic performance of this composition, when does an infringement exist?" [8]

Bronzo offered a three-part answer:

- If there is no accompanying dialogue, scenery, costumes, and the like, it is a nondramatic rendition.

- If it "(1) occurs within an overall performance possessing a definite plot, and (2) the rendition is an integral part of *that* plot, *i.e.*, 'helps to tell the story,' " it is a dramatic rendition.

- If dramatic material from the work accompanies it, a non-instrumental selection is dramatic. [9]

According to Boxer, "what makes a song dramatic rests in the discretion of the judge" because infringement is determined by judicial decision NOT congressional legislation. [10]

Another approach to distinguishing between dramatic and nondramatic musical performances is to determine whether *grand* or *small performing rights* are required. **Grand rights** allow the performance of music in a dramatic fashion. They are obtained from the copyright owner or from licensing agencies such as Tams-Witmark Music Library, Rodgers & Hammerstein Library, Music Theatre International, and Samuel French, Inc. (see Appendix A for addresses). In 1981, their cost ranged from $100 per song per performance week to a percentage of the gross weekly box office receipts.

Small rights allow the nondramatic performance of music. The American Society of Composers, Authors & Publishers (ASCAP), Broadcast Music, Inc. (BMI), or SESAC usually handles these rights which include live performances, playing a record, broadcasting a live or recorded performance, and rebroadcasting such a broadcasted performance. [11] Most TV and radio stations, nightclubs, discos, universities, restaurants, and sports stadiums hold musical performance licenses from all of these organizations. Often these are blanket licenses renewed annually, thus avoiding the need for individual permission to perform each song. Siegel suggested that those hiring groups to perform in "quasi-profit" settings such as a corporation's Christmas dinner, should ask the establishment where the performance will take place if it has licensing agreements with ASCAP, BMI, and SESAC. Otherwise, the company might be liable for the licenses. [12]

In other words,

> if you perform "Yesterday" in a piano-bar . . . , John Lennon
> and Paul McCartney [and Michael Jackson since he now
> owns the copyright] theoretically receive their share of the
> bar owner's license fee in compensation. If you include
> "Yesterday" in a film however, or a stage play or as
> background music for a commercial, you must obtain a
> proper license. [13]

Or, as Boxer recommended

> [T]he producer of a television show should always apply the
> following rule of thumb: when the television show
> contains musical compositions, whether or not taken from
> any type of play or dramatic composition, and the
> composition is woven into the television "sketch," procure
> the consent of the copyright proprietor of the dramatico-
> musical or musical composition to use his work in such a
> manner. The amount paid to the copyright proprietor is
> negligible compared to the possibility of future litigation. [14]

Two court cases illustrate the problem of differentiating
between dramatic and nondramatic performance. *The Robert
Stigwood Group v. Sperber* was one of the approximately ten cases
over the rock opera *Jesus Christ Superstar.* *Gershwin v. The Whole
Thing Company* dealt with a musical play entitled *Let's Call the Whole
Thing Gershwin.*

In *Stigwood v. Sperber,* the Robert Stigwood Group, which
owned the stage production and dramatic presentation rights to
Jesus Christ Superstar, sought to prevent Betty Sperber and her
companies from performing twenty of the opera's twenty-three songs
and from referring to the opera in their advertisements. Sperber
claimed her productions were not infringements because Leeds
Music Corp. which handled the music had the usual agreement with
ASCAP.

In affirming the lower court's injunction against Sperber, Judge Kaufman wrote for the Second Circuit:

ASCAP is authorized by its members to license only nondramatic performing rights of compositions in its repertory [because it was felt] that each copyright owner could appropriately police and license performances of musical comedies or operas because of the relative infrequency of such productions and the lengthy preparation and publicity which must precede these productions. [15]

So the question facing the court is whether Sperber's performances were dramatic or nondramatic. The court held that "the lack of scenery or costumes . . . does not *ipso facto* prevent it from being dramatic . . . . Indeed, radio performances of operas are considered dramatic, because the story is told by the music and lyrics." [16]

Thus, the court found no question that Sperber's concerts were dramatic. It modified the preliminary injunction to prevent further infringement saying that once a prima facie case of infringement has been made, a preliminary injunction is needed even if detailed showing of irreparable harm is not shown because copyright owners of dramatico-musical works are harmed when their exclusive use is invaded. But contrast this decision with *April Productions v. Strand* where the court held that a medley of songs from a musical play included in one scene of a nightclub show was a nondramatic performance under ASCAP's licensing agreement. [17]

In *Gershwin v. The Whole Thing Company*, Ira Gershwin sought and won a preliminary injunction against The Whole Thing Company. The defendant produced a musical play capitalizing on the popularity of Gershwin's music and lyrics. The company obtained the appropriate copyright license from the music publishers and Mr. Gershwin. Gershwin's license permitted the play to be performed only at the Westwood Playhouse and only until January 31, 1980. The Whole Thing Company, however, continued presenting the play after that date.

The defendant originally obtained licenses from music publishers but not Ira Gershwin. When Gershwin found out in 1979, he informed the defendant that a license from him was required because "the music publishers did not possess sufficient rights of copyright for the dramatic live stage production . . . and because Mr. Gershwin's right of publicity would be invaded." [18] A settlement was reached and the license granted to January 31, 1980. A request for an extension to take the show to Broadway was denied.

The court found that Gershwin showed substantial evidence of the possibility of irreparable harm and was entitled to relief. Also, the court found that Gershwin basically granted small performing rights (i.e., non-dramatic rights) to the music publishers and retained the grand performing rights (i.e., dramatic rights).

OBTAINING PROPERTY RIGHTS

Thus, in dealing with dramatic and dramatico-musical works, you want to obtain the grand rights to the work. You can find previously produced playwrights through the Dramatists Guild. The Writers Guild and Copyright Office also may help.

If the play was previously produced, one of the play licensing companies may list it in its catalogue. For example, the Tams-Witmark Music Library acquired the rights to many Broadway musicals.[19] The Rodgers and Hammerstein Library handles the stock and amateur stage performance rights for various musical plays. Royalties are calculated on an individual basis from information provided by the producer. [20]

When you negotiate your contract for performance rights, be sure you cover all aspects. As boxed notices throughout the 1985 Samuel French catalogue announce: "Royalty quotes in our catalogue are for LIVE STAGED PRODUCTIONS ONLY. No other rights are therein granted. No Television, Film Video or Audio Recording may be made of your production at any time." Other notices declare: "Terms for mechanical rights for radio broadcasting, television, professional performances, for public, or private readings, etc., will be quoted on application." And still other notices advise: "Special arrangement must in all cases be made for professional, motion picture, recitation, public reading, radio broadcasting, television, cable television, public television, and the rights of translation into foreign language." Thus, for example, if you want to videotape a community theater group's theatrical production for playback on the local access channel, you would need to specifically ask before taping for the right to perform the play with video playback on the access channel. You do not tape the production and then request permission. [21]

Apropos of fair use, William Talbot, editor-in-chief at Samuel French, Inc. remarked:

[I]t is our belief that fair use of copyrighted dramas by producers of film, video and multi-image forms would be an impossibility, and any attempts to exercise the putative right of fair use in such instances would present an insuperable onus of proof on such producers. Drama is an emotional art, and each enactment before any audience diminishes the total potential audience for, and hence the value of, every drama. [22]

If you still doubt the stringency with which copyright on dramatic works is protected, check The New York Public Library's Theatre on Film and Tape Collection's "Conditions of November 12, 1970." For example, it requires applying in advance to see a work and bans reproductions in any form. [23]

REFERENCES

1. *Senate*, p. 52; *House*, pp. 53-54.
2. Vincent Louis Perrone, "Small and Grand Performing Rights? (Who Cared Before 'Jesus Christ Superstar')", *Bulletin of the Copyright Society of the U.S.A.* 20 (1972-73): 21-22.

3. *Nimmer on Copyright*, §2.06[A].
4. *Nimmer*, §2.06[A].
5. *Nimmer*, §2.06[C].
6. Lester Boxer, "Dramatic Performing Rights in Dramatico-Musical Compositions," *Southern California Law Review* 34 (1961): 448.
7. 177 F. 287, 287 (S.D.N.Y. 1909).
8. Boxer, p. 453; see also *Nimmer*, §2.06[D].
9. John F. Bronzo, "Copyright—Infringement of Dramatico-Musical Rights—ASCAP License—*Robert Stigwood Group Ltd. v. Sperber,*" *Boston College Industrial and Commercial Law Review* 14 (1972-1973): 1310.
10. Boxer, p. 449.
11. For a description of how these agencies work see, for example, H. Finkelstein, "ASCAP As an Example of the Clearing House System in Operation," *Bulletin of the Copyright Society of the U.S.A.* 14 (1966): 2-7; Gertz, Van Petten, and Van Petten, pp. 3-92; and Sinofsky, pp. 95-97.
12. Richard J. Siegel, "Non-Profit Musical Performance Societies and the 1976 Copyright Act," *Northern Illinois University Law Review* 2 (Spring 1982): 462-463.
13. Thomas R. Leavens, "Performing Arts & the Law," in *Law and the Arts—Art and the Law* (Chicago: Lawyers for the Creative Arts, 1979), p. 50.
14. Boxer, p. 463.
15. 457 F.2d 50, 52 (2d Cir. 1972).
16. 457 F.2d 50, 55 (2d Cir. 1972).
17. 221 F.2d 292 (2d Cir. 1955).
18. 208 U.S.P.Q. 557, 558 (C.D. Cal. 1980).
19. Michael I. Rudell, *Behind the Scenes: Practical Entertainment Law* (New York: Law & Business/Harcourt Brace Jovanovich, 1984), p. 161.
20. Charles Mathes, Director, letter, 7 June 1985.
21. Ernest T. Sanchez, *Copyright and You* (Washington, DC: National Federation of Local Cable Programmers, n.d.), pp. 11-12.
22. Letter, 29 May 1985.
23. Betty L. Corwin, Director, letter, 28 May 1985.

CHAPTER   12:

VISUALS   AND   TALENT

As noted in Chapter 10, once you have your script, title, and character rights, you simply cannot go out and begin photographing. (For the purposes of this chapter, **photography** is used in its broadest sense to include **video** and **filming**.)   Identifiable people, objects, and locations require permission for inclusion in your production. This chapter looks at photography: who owns what rights; what and whom can be photographed; and how to obtain copyrighted visuals.

WHO OWNS THE RIGHTS?

Ownership of rights is a basic concern of copyright law. Copyright owners can do as they please with their works; users are extremely limited in what they can do with a copyrighted work.   So the first question that arises is who owns the photograph (or slide or film or the like)?   Under the 1909 Act, the employer or client owned the photograph. [1]   Under the 1976 Act, the photographer owns the photograph.

For example, a commercial photographer specializing in corporate annual reports told me that a company used one of his photographs of the firm in an advertisement without his permission. He notified them that their use of his photograph was unauthorized and compensation was required.   The company had not known about the change in the copyright law.   The issue was settled out of court—at the cost of several thousand dollars to the company.

In other words, under current copyright law, if you hire an outside photographer, you probably are buying one-time usage rights. If you want additional rights, negotiate them when you first hire the photographer. In-house photographers, like in-house writers and designers, usually fall under the "work-for-hire" category, so their employers own the rights to their work.

THE RIGHT TO PHOTOGRAPH

Your right to take pictures is not the same as your right to use those pictures (the latter is discussed in the next section). In a studio, your right to take pictures is generally governed by local ordinances covering issues such as negligence. Out on the street, you are free to take as many pictures as you want as long as you do not interfere with traffic or invade someone's privacy. According to *Pagano v. Charles Beseler Co.*, anyone may take a photograph of a public building and its surrounding scene. But it is the originality used in determining when to take the photograph, how to light or shade it, and the like that makes it copyrightable. [2]

In *Galella v. Onassis*, Ronald E. Galella brought an action against Jackie Onassis and three secret service agents for false arrest, malicious prosecution, and interference with trade.

Galella, a free-lance "paparazzo" specializing in photos of the famous, jumped into the path of John Jr.'s bicycle, causing alarm. There were also several other incidents by the time Mrs. Onassis counterclaimed assault and battery, invasion of privacy, intentional infliction of emotional distress, and harassment by Galella.

The court agreed that Onassis was a public figure and therefore a subject for news coverage. But, the court found Galella's actions beyond reasonable bounds "when weighed against the *de minimus* public importance of the daily activities of the defendant." [3] To Galella's claim of First Amendment immunity for newsmen gathering news, the court responded: "There is no such scope to the First Amendment rights. Crimes and torts committed in news gathering are not protected." Furthermore, "there is no threat to a free press in requiring its agents to act within the law." [4] The complaint was dismissed and injunctive relief granted to Jackie Onassis.

Museums, theaters, sports arenas, stadiums, concert halls, hospitals, and even restaurants may restrict photography. For example, a museum may be involved in a question of who owns the copyright in a work. This may lead to restrictions on photographing works, including photographs in catalogues, and selling reproductions in the museum shop.

Le Mistral v. CBS involved a restaurant's right to restrict photography. On July 6, 1972, a CBS reporter and camera crew were directed to visit some restaurants cited for New York City health code violations. The CBS team entered the premises with the camera "rolling" and bright camera lights. They did not seek an appointment or permission to enter. They were asked to leave.

Many patrons were upset: those waiting, left; some left without paying their checks; and others hid their faces. Even by their own admission, the CBS employees were guilty of trespass. Thus, the jury concluded that the CBS employees, bursting into the "restaurant in [a] noisy and obstrusive fashion," were guilty of trespass and awarded the plaintiff compensatory and punitive damages.

CBS claimed First Amendment protection from the damage award despite its trespass. But, the court commented: "the First Amendment is not a shibboleth before which all other rights must succumb." [5] That is, freedom of the press is not threatened by requiring reporters to act within the law.

Other areas where photographic restrictions apply include U.S. military and naval installations, currency, securities, and postage stamps. While black and white photographs of currency, securities, and stamps for "philatelic, numismatic, educational, historical or newsworthy purposes" [6] may be permitted, restrictions exist on color reproductions. Permission is needed from the Secretary of the Treasury because of counterfeiting concerns. Courtrooms also fall under various restrictions. These vary from state to state.

THE RIGHT TO USE A PHOTOGRAPH

While you have the right to photograph almost anything, you do not automatically have the right to sell, display, or reproduce that photograph. If you use a person's name, image, or likeness—or in some instances a person's pet or property—without that person's permission, you risk a lawsuit. These lawsuits generally deal with the right of privacy. Some legal commentators, though, differentiate between private and public figures. Private people, they maintain, come under the right of privacy; public figures, under the right of publicity.

The doctrine of privacy evolved at the state rather than the federal level. Several states have legislation on the books, most notably New York's Civil Rights Law Sections 50-51 and California's Civil Code Section 3344. In many other states, the courts have held that the right of privacy does exist.

Selz and Simensky identified four types of invasion of privacy: (1) intrusion into private affairs; (2) public disclosure of embarrassing private facts; (3) publicity placing a person in a false light in the public eye; and (4) appropriation of a person's name or likeness for advantage. The first three types prevent personal and emotional harm; the last protects the person's commercial interests. Thus privacy claims consist of three parts: (1) the use of a person's name, image, or likeness (2) without consent (3) for another's commercial benefit. [7] The bottom line is to prevent the exploitation of people without their consent.

How do you know if you can use a photograph? In *Lahiri v. Daily Mirror*, Justice Shientag formulated the basic rules of thumb for deciding if a photograph is an invasion of privacy. It may be an invasion of privacy if used commercially or to illustrate a work of fiction. It may not invade a person's privacy if used in connection with a current news item or is educational or informative in character. [8] In other words, you can use the photograph if you have the person's permission. You cannot use it for commercial purposes without the person's permission. And any other use that is not obscene or libelous is a "maybe." As always, the answers depend upon the facts of the case in question.

For example, in *Arrington v. The New York Times*, Arrington's photograph was taken without his permission and used as the cover illustration for a feature article on the Black middle class. Though his name was not used, he objected to the association with the author's position. The *New York Times* was not held liable. [9]

But what about photographing students or employees and using these pictures without their consent for promotional purposes or to illustrate an article? I have not found such a case, but it would not be unreasonable. Obtaining consent to use those pictures could save you time, money, and aggravation.

Permission to use a person's name, image, or likeness should be in writing. The best way of obtaining this written consent is to have the person (a parent or guardian in the case of a minor) sign a release at the time you take the picture. Trying to find people later is not only difficult, but can cause costly production delays.

A release is simply written consent stating that the person being photographed allows this photograph to be taken and subsequently used. Unfortunately, there are no standard release or model release forms as they are called (see Appendix B3 for sources of sample releases) and those available are often inadequate. When you develop your release, try to be specific:

> Give a timetable for permissible publication. List the actual uses to which you intend to put the material. Include language to the effect that the pictures or tape might be used "in whole or in part, composite or distorted, in conjunction with your own or a fictitious name . . . " and so on. [10]

Too broad a release might work against you in court. Giving a copy of the signed release to the person is also a good idea.

In *Welch v. Mr. Christmas*, Charles C. Welch, a professional actor, sued Mr. Christmas, Inc., a manufacturer of artificial Christmas trees, for invasion of privacy. Welch's contract with Mr.

Christmas was for one year, with an option for one more year, with a $1,000 fee for a TV commercial advertising the defendant's product. Despite a caution delivered through the Screen Actors Guild (SAG), the commercial was shown an additional year. Since the contract's (that is, the written consent's) time limit on use had expired, the additional use was considered an invasion of privacy. The trial court awarded Welch $1,000 in compensatory and $15,000 in punitive damages. The decision was affirmed by the New York Supreme Court. [11]

If Vanessa Williams had signed a more specific release, she might have prevented *Penthouse*'s publication of her pictures and retained her Miss America crown. Or, if Dale Bozzio, Missing Person's vocalist, had signed a more specific release, she might have prevented *Hustler*'s publication of a five-page pictorial spread.

If you decide to use professionals for your shots, you not only need a model release or a contract (in the case of actors and actresses), but need to consider the costs. A top professional model may cost up to $300 per hour. The Screen Actors Guild (SAG) and the American Federation of Television and Radio Artists (AFTRA) [12] set the basic rate schedule for professional actors and actresses. Contrary to popular myth, there is currently no mandatory agent's commission. These rates change as the groups renegotiate their contracts (at the time of writing, a new contract is being negotiated). Here are some sample figures based on 1984 and 1985 rates:

- SAG offers a special $275 per day actor contract for educational videos. There is also a special student production contract.

- There is no charge for an audition and one callback; but, a second callback runs approximately $80. An audition longer than an hour costs around $40.

- A session fee (that is, eight hours of work excluding lunch) will cost you around $320 per actor and $211 per extra. Add $10 for each outfit you ask them to bring. Overtime runs around $60 per hour ($40 for an extra) for the first two hours; around $80 per hour ($53 for an extra) after the tenth hour of work.

But what if the person is dead? Is it an invasion of privacy to reproduce his/her likeness? As early as 1894, courts found themselves facing this question. In that year, Emily A. Corliss sued to enjoin the E. W. Walker Company from inserting a portrait of George H. Corliss into a biographical sketch it wanted to publish. Circuit Judge Colt concluded: "[The] question resolves itself into ... how far an individual, in his lifetime, or his heirs at law after his death, have the right to control the reproduction of his picture or photograph." Furthermore, "a private individual has a right to be protected in the representation of his portrait in any form; that this is a property as well as a personal right." [13] However, since Corliss had been a public figure of the era, the court granted the defendant's motion to dissolve the injunction against publishing the portrait.

In recent years, cases involving the privacy and/or publicity rights of dead actors and singers have flourished. Generally, whether a person's right of publicity continues after his/her death depends on where the lawsuit is brought. Some states passed legislation limiting the right of publicity to twenty to fifty years after death—much like copyright's current duration. In California, such a law only covers people who register their celebrityhood with the Secretary of State.

In *Lugosi v. Universal Pictures*, Lugosi's heirs wanted to stop the use of Dracula on T-shirts and other merchandise. The California Supreme Court decided that the actor's heirs could not assert the dead actor's right to control the commercialization of his likeness: "[T]he right to exploit name and likeness is personal to the artist and must be exercised if at all, by him during his lifetime." [14] However, the court observed that if Lugosi had exploited his likeness during his lifetime, he could have impressed a secondary meaning upon it protectible under the law of unfair competition.

Similarly, in several cases involving Elvis Presley's name, the Sixth Circuit ruled that celebrities' exclusive rights to profit from their name and likeness does not continue after death. [15] But, in *Factors Etc. v. Pro Arts*, the Court held Presley's right of publicity continued after his death since he exercised it during his life. [16]

What of *living* public figures? There is a fine line between reproducing pictures of public figures for informative as opposed to commercial purposes. In the latter case the person's "right of publicity" is being abused. In *Paulsen v. Personality Posters Inc.*, comedian Pat Paulsen tried to sue a distributor of posters featuring his picture with the words "For President." Though Pat Paulsen's 1968 presidential campaign was tongue-in-cheek, the court considered it newsworthy and of public interest. Therefore, the Paulsen presidential posters were considered a public interest presentation worthy of protection. Paulsen discovered what many politicians already know: there is little right of publicity for people in the political arena. [17]

Joe Namath tried to sue *Sports Illustrated* when it used one of its previously published Namath pictures in a subscription solicitation campaign. Since the ads did not imply endorsement, Namath lost: "[The] photograph was merely incidental advertising of defendant's magazine in which plaintiff had earlier been properly and fairly depicted . . . ." [18] Similarly in *Booth v. Curtis Publishing*, well-known actress Shirley Booth lost her invasion of privacy suit against Curtis, the publisher of *Holiday*, for subsequently using pictures of her published in *Holiday* for ads in *Advertising Age* and the *New Yorker*. [19] Notice, though, that both *Sports Illustrated* and *Holiday* used previously published pictures they already had the right to publish.

REPRODUCING COPYRIGHTED VISUALS

There are several sources for ready-made production visuals: fair use, picture agencies, stock houses, and archives.

Fair Use

Fair use reproduction of audiovisual works has never been fully resolved by Congress. A. Brian Helm claimed: "A single copy *of a portion* [emphasis in original] of a copyrighted film or filmstrip [or slide program] may be made by a student for educational purposes if the material *is owned* [emphasis in original] by the school which the student is attending." But, he went on to caution that extreme care must be exercised because the portion, however small, "may contain the very essence of the material in question." [20] Taking the "very essence" would be copyright infringement.   Becker followed a 10% rule.   For example, he submitted the following as permissible uses:

1. Creating a series of slides from multiple sources, such as magazines, books, encyclopedias, etc. as long as one doesn't exceed 10% of the photographs in any one source, unless the source specifically prohibits any photographic reproduction.

. . . .

4. Excerpting sections from a filmstrip to create slides as long as one doesn't exceed 10% of the entire work or excerpt the very creative essence of the work.[21]

Since most publishers and producers usually place a comprehensive statement prohibiting all types of copying next to their copyright notice, Becker's first example would probably cover only a few sources.   And, since the portion copied would probably be the "very essence," copying under either Helm's or Becker's rules would be extremely hard to defend.   Also, the 10% rule of thumb does not seem to be supported by the literature.

Carl May of Biological Photo Services explained:

Regarding fair use, I personally have never had qualms about a photo appearing casually in another larger picture —for example as a hanging on a background wall or on the cover of a book someone is reading.   However, if a photo is the primary information viewed at any point in time, then its use should be covered by permission.   An image is someone's property; just as one is not free to use a stranger's automobile for a short trip down the road without asking, one is not free to use a photographer's creation for one's own purposes.

By arrangement with our scientist-photographers, all of whom still own the materials stocked with our agencies and retain the copyright to the images, I can never allow the use of a stock photo without a compensatory fee. When someone like an educator or charitable organization requests free use of a photo, I relay the request to the photographer involved. Because most of our photographers are educators as well, they will usually grant permission for reasonable uses without a fee. When asked for advice on educational requests, I usually suggest that the photographer consider whether or not the desired use is strictly local, strictly limited in terms of time and number of copies, and *free* [emphasis in original] to the student. [22]

The following three cases involved film clips and fair use. As you will see, in each case the defendant was accused of copyright infringement, claimed fair use, and lost the case.

In *Iowa State University Research Foundation v. American Broadcasting Companies*, Iowa State alleged that ABC infringed its copyright in a student-produced film about Dan Gable, an Olympic wrestler. The district court found ABC liable for copyright infringement through two unauthorized showings of portions of Iowa State's film on national TV during ABC's 1972 Olympic games coverage. But the court found no copying involved in ABC's independently created film on the same subject matter.

How did ABC find itself in this predicament? James Doran and another Iowa State student produced *Champion*, an approximately twenty-eight-minute long sports biography film of Iowa State's champion wrestler Dan Gable who went on to win a gold medal at the 1972 Munich Olympics. As most works of this genre, it included shots of Gable at home, on campus, wrestling, interviews with his family, teammates, and Gable himself. The film was copyrighted in 1971. Iowa State gave Doran the right to negotiate the first TV showing—but only with the university's full consent and knowledge. Doran tried to interest commercial stations but was unsuccessful.

In 1972, while working as a videotape operator and filer for ABC Sports, he overheard two ABC Sports producers discussing the lack of background film on Gable. Doran mentioned *Champion* and gave one producer a copy to view. Unknown to Doran, ABC copied the entire tape and used almost three minutes of it in its 1972 Olympic coverage (a 7-12 second segment in Olympic previews and a 2 1/2-minute segment during the games). Doran never informed ABC of Iowa State's restrictions, nor Iowa State of ABC's interest. ABC, furthermore, had already decided to send out its own crew.

While watching the games, Doran saw the fragments and contacted ABC and then Iowa State. Though ABC did not know of Doran's contractual limitations, Iowa State's copyright notice was on the film and Doran never gave permission for its use without payment.

The court found ABC's fair use claim lacked merit. The court pointed out that since Doran originally tried to sell the film, ABC knew some payment was expected. Also, since ABC sent a crew to Iowa, that proves it considered the topic of some value. But, the court found ABC's independently produced seven-minute clip on Gable typical of its genre and thus not an infringement of *Champion*. [23]

In affirming the lower court's decision, Chief Judge Kaufman (writing for the Second Circuit) expanded upon ABC's claim of fair use. Section 107 does not apply here because Iowa State's copyright was from before the 1976 Act took effect. Fair use, "originally created and articulated in case law, permits courts to avoid rigid application of the copyright statute when, on occasion, it would stifle the very creativity which that law is designed to foster." [24] He rejected ABC's public benefit argument saying ABC could use the factual information to enlighten its audience but could not appropriate Iowa State's expression of that information. Also, ABC was interested in commercial exploitation, not just the public benefit.

Roy Export Company v. Columbia Broadcasting System focused on a film clip of Charlie Chaplin film highlights. Roy Export owned the copyright in and various distribution rights to the six Charlie Chaplin films highlighted: *The Kid, The Gold Rush, The Circus, City Lights, Modern Times,* and *The Great Dictator.* In 1972, the Academy of Motion Picture Arts and Sciences (AMPAS) wanted to give Chaplin a special award during the Academy Awards show. It asked Bert Schneider (who was authorized to act for two of the plaintiffs) to "supervise the preparation of a tribute to Chaplin consisting of highlights from the Chaplin films." [25] The team put together a thirteen-minute film of Chaplin film highlights which was shown on the 1972 Academy Awards telecast. Schneider's contract with AMPAS authorized only one broadcast.

Between 1974 and 1975, Roy Export authorized the use of many of the same highlights for a film biography of Chaplin, *The Gentleman Tramp*, a ninety-minute special, designed for U.S. TV.

In 1973, CBS began work on its own Chaplin retrospective program. It requested permission to use the film excerpts, but was refused because of the film the plaintiff was producing. CBS prepared a "rough cut" including two scenes obtained for use in 1972 for "60 Minutes."

In 1976 and 1977, the plaintiff tried to sell licenses for *The Gentleman Tramp* to CBS. On December 25, 1977, Chaplin died. CBS tried getting permission to use excerpts. It received a copy of the 1972 clip from NBC, but could not reach the plaintiff. CBS had two versions of its Chaplin retrospective for broadcast: one consisted primarily of public domain footage; the other was based on the 1972 clip and consisted of forty percent of Roy Export's copyrighted films. CBS used the latter version.

CBS maintained that the motion should be dismissed because:

(1) its use of the copyrighted works was protected as a matter of law by the fair use doctrine or the First Amendment to the Constitution; (2) plaintiffs had no common law copyright interest in any work in issue; (3) the common law unfair competition claim was federally preempted by the copyright statutes in this case; and (4) its use of two of the copyright works was authorized as a matter of law. [26]

After a three week trial, the jury found that CBS infringed Roy Export's statutory and common law copyrights and had unfairly competed. The jury awarded Roy Export over $700,000 in damages and compensation.

Affirming the lower court's decision, the Second Circuit noted that the 1976 Act eliminated, for most purposes, the distinction between common-law and statutory copyright. Questions still arise regarding pre-1978 (1976 Act effective January 1, 1978) common law protection for intellectual property. CBS was found liable for $307,281 in compensatory and $410,000 in punitive damages and $5,000 additional award of statutory damages.

Addressing CBS's First Amendment defense, the court remarked:

> No Circuit that has considered the question, however, has ever held that the First Amendment provides a privilege in the copyright field distinct from the accommodation embodied in the "fair use" doctrine. [27]

Regarding common-law copyright, the court found a problem with the meaning of *publication*. The plaintiff claimed AMPAS's showing of the film clip was a performance not a publication. The court explained:

> It is axiomatic that copyright is a protection for an *original* [emphasis in original] work . . . . Without an assignment from the proprietor of a component, the compiler of a collective work cannot secure copyright protection for preexisting components that he did not create; protection is available only for that part of his product that is original with him—for what he has added to the component works, or for his skill and creativity in selecting and assembling an original arrangement of those works, even if no new material is added. [28]

As for unfair competition, the court found CBS's use falls under the New York state law. Therefore, the court affirmed the district court's decision.

Pacific & Southern Company v. Duncan dealt with a TV news clipping service. The plaintiff, Pacific & Southern, does business as WXIA-TV. The defendant, Carol Duncan, does business as TV News Clips. The TV station brought charges against the TV news clipping service over a one minute forty-five second feature story on the addition of various athletic devices to a jogging path at Floyd Junior College (Rome, GA) called the "fitness trail."

According to Chief Judge Orinola Evans: "This case presents the question whether off the air video taping of live television news broadcasts by a TV news monitoring service, followed by the marketing and sale of news tapes to interested members of the public, infringes the broadcaster's copyright under federal law." [29]

WXIA had not developed a news clips market. When asked, it would charge $100 per copy but did not provide the service for everyone. For example, it did not provide the service for politicians because it was afraid the clip would be used in a campaign. The perceived need for purchasing such video clips was to study and improve the image projected to the public. Also, lawyers sometimes wanted a story relevant to a case. A few just wanted souvenirs.

Looking at the issue of statutory protection for copyright and TV news, the court noted:

It is axiomatic that copyright protection does not extend to news "events" or the facts or ideas which are the subject of news reports . . . . But it is equally well-settled that copyright protection does extend to the reports themselves, as distinguished from the substance of the information contained in the reports. [30]

Duncan's copying does not merely relate the substance, it reproduces both the facts and how they were presented. So WXIA is entitled to judgment in its favor unless Duncan's First Amendment and fair use defenses are meritorious.

Duncan argued that "an unlimited copyright in television news violates the First Amendment." She pointed to the public's interest in the fullest dissemination and "the unique ephemeral nature of television news broadcasts." [31] TV stations do not have to preserve broadcast materials, nor do they have to make copies readily available.

The court said that the tension between copyright and First Amendment issues are usually settled by fair use or the idea-expression dichotomy. However, sometimes the idea and expression are impossible to separate and the work of such public interest that an unauthorized use may be fair as in the case of the My Lai massacre photographs and Zapruder's movie of John F. Kennedy's assassination. But, the court did not think it applied here.

The court rejected the fair use defense because Duncan's use did not resemble any listed under Section 107. In a note discussing the Section 108(f) exemption, the court commented: "Comparative advertisement, like satire, is a productive and creative use of the copyrighted material. Ms. Duncan's copying and distribution, on the other hand, was not an inherently productive or creative use of the type referred to in §107." [32]

The court did not favor broad injunctive relief because WXIA erased tapes within a week and Duncan within a month. Thus, Duncan might be providing a small social benefit. Since the feature was an unpublished work and Duncan made $35 profit, the court ordered Duncan to pay WXIA the $35.

On appeal, the Eleventh Circuit affirmed in part and reversed in part. It held that Duncan's activities did not constitute fair use and were infringing. Therefore, the plaintiff was entitled to a permanent injunction. It criticized the lower court for not looking at the fair use criteria: "Fair use allows a court to resolve tensions between the ends of the copyright law, public enjoyment of creative works, and . . . the conferral of economic benefits upon creators of original works." [33] It also found that TV News Clips competed with WXIA's potential market since it copied the entire work.

A related ready-made visuals issue stems from copyright's protection of photographic prints from unauthorized copying in *other media* as well. This protection was established as early as 1888 in *Falk v. T. P. Howell & Co.* Falk claimed his copyrighted photograph of Geraldine Ulmer as Yum Yum in the *Mikado* was infringed when Howell stamped its likeness on leather used for chair bottoms and backs. The court decided this was an infringement because "differences which relate merely to size and material are not important." [34] This occurs more frequently than you may think. Graphic artists and others often "copy and/or 'strip out' the whole or a substantial part of a photograph for use in their designs, paintings, posters, and other visual art without permission of the photographer." [35]

Picture Agencies and Stock Houses

Cavallo and Kahan defined a **stock agency** (or stock library or stock house or picture agency) as "an organization which handles photographs in bulk" and desires "to sell a product rather than simply a service." [36] However, though both picture agencies and stock houses provide visuals for productions, they do so in different ways.

Picture agencies do exactly what their name implies: they act as middlemen between photographers and clients. Like other agents, they receive a percentage of the photographer's fee in return for generating assignments and handling business and administrative matters. In other words, picture agencies handle specific photographers for specific assignments. These assignments usually cover annual reports, industrial photography, public relations, and still and motion picture work.

Stock houses usually handle freelance work. These visuals are often seen in travel brochures, calendars, plaques, posters, greeting cards, books, and TV spot advertising.

Current rates and rights in stock and assignment photography are listed in sources such as *Professional Business Practices* by the

Figure 12.1 Sample Rate Sheet   Chapter Twelve VISUALS AND TALENT

Biological Photo Service
P.O. Box 490
Moss Beach, California 94038
(415) 726-6244

Stock Photos by Professional Biologists
Photo Research for the Life Sciences

TEXTBOOK RATES FOR STOCK PHOTOGRAPHS

(Rates for other uses available by phone)

	1/8 page or less	to 1/2 page	to full page	two-page spread	cover or jacket
BLACK AND WHITE	$55	70	100	175	150 up
COLOR	$80	100	150	250	250 up

1. Prices effective as of November 1, 1983, and may be changed without notice.

2. All prices cover world rights in the English language and are for use one time in one edition.

3. Page rates quoted are for editorial use. For chapter openers, unit openers, end sheets, frontispiece, or other design uses, add 25% to appropriate rate.

4. The charge for each additional language will be 20% of the above rates. One-time, one-edition world rights in all languages may be obatined for twice the above rates.

5. Charges for covers and jackets to be determined by size. Charges for small photos used in composites may be lower than the above cover rates.

6. In new editions, charge for use of same photo, same size, in same format will be 70% of original.

DISCOUNTS

- 10% for use of more than 10 photos in same title.
- 15% for use of more than 25 photos in same title.
Rates negotiable for illustration of entire texts or major sections of texts.

RESEARCH

No research fees are charged for stock photos.
Special research is available for all biological subjects not in stock.

American Society of Magazine Photographers (ASMP). Rates for freelance photographers can range from $150 a day for black and white work ($300 a day for color) to $1000 a day plus expenses for top photographers. [37] Life Picture Service, which provides copies of photographs used in *Life*, charges a service fee for handling requests of $100 per hour which may be waived or reduced if the photograph is used. Also, due to agreements with its photographers, Life Picture Service charges a minimum license fee of $150. [38] Figure 12.1 presents a sample rate sheet for textbook visuals.

Visuals from such agencies and houses may be costly, but they come complete with the appropriate rights—saving you possible court appearances.[39] To find a stock agency or library near you, check the following sources: *Creative Black Book*; *Art Director's Index*; *Working Press of the Nation*; Jerome K. Miller's *The Copyright Directory, Volume I*; *Picture Researcher's Handbook: An International Guide to Picture Sources—and How to Use Them* (3rd ed.); and the Special Libraries Association's *Picture Sources* (4th ed.).

Archives

Need a visual of an ancient artifact? medieval map? authentic illustration? You might consider archives, research collections, and museums. Since many of their materials are in the public domain, you avoid copyright, liable, and invasion of privacy problems. Also, though they charge for prints and reproduction fees, their invoice may amount to only one-tenth of a photo agency's bill. In addition to previously mentioned sources, you might check Hoffberg & Hess's *Directory of Art Libraries and Visual Collections in North America* for resources near you.

James Cross Giblin described his use of such sources when searching for illustrations for his book, *Walls: Defenses Throughout History*. For his chapter on World War II, he found thirty-two possibilities by contacting the French and West German consulate information offices; following a lead to the Hoover Institute (Stanford, CA); visiting the National Archives, the Library of Congress' Prints and Photographs Division, the New York Public Library's Picture Collection; and writing the Imperial War Museum

(Great Britain).   In the end, he used thirteen of these illustrations. Total cost: $135. [40]

On the other hand, Maxine Fleckner Ducey, Director of the Film Archive, Wisconsin Center for Film and Theater Research, explained they will provide a copy of a film still for research purposes only.

> The researcher must contact the copyright holder for permission to publish. We charge no reproduction fees, nor do we provide copyright information . . . . [W]e require written permission from the copyright holder *and the donor* [emphasis in original] of the film. This applies to all duplication, whether for classroom use or otherwise. [41]

Thus, while you might locate a particular film, motion picture and TV film clips may be difficult to obtain.   They are definitely expensive to clear.   As Ducey noted, you need clearance from the clip's copyright owner—usually a motion picture studio.   Most studios consider clips unprofitable and bothersome so they often say "No."   If they say "yes," be prepared to pay between $3,600 and $30,000 or more per *minute* for the clip.   Guilds' and unions' fees and royalties may also affect film clip rights.   In addition, you need a release from all those identifiable in the clip.   And, depending on SAG and AFTRA agreements, fees for reruns may be involved. Music adds the cost of paying each musician and clearing the underlying musical rights. [42]

REFERENCES

1. See, for example, *Lumiere v. Pathe Exchange*, 275 F. 428 (2d Cir. 1921); *Lumiere v. Robertson-Cole Distributing Corp.*, 280 F. 550 (2d Cir. 1922); *Colten v. Jacques Marchais*, 61 N.Y.S.2d 269 (N.Y. Mun. Ct. 1946); and *Avedon v. Exstein*, 141 F. Supp. 278 (S.D.N.Y. 1956).
2. 234 F. 963 (S.D.N.Y. 1916).
3. 1 Med. L. Rptr. 2425, 2429 (2d Cir. 1973).
4. 1 Med. L. Rptr. 2425, 2429-2430 (2d Cir. 1973).
5. 3 Med. L. Rptr. 1913, 1914 (N.Y. App. Div. 1978).
6. George Chernoff and Hershel Sarbin, *Photography and the Law* (New York: Amphoto, 1977), pp. 5-6.
7. §§18.01; 18.04.
8. 162 Misc. 776 (1937).
9. 55 NY2d 433 (Ct. App. 1982).
10. Kathleen Lane, "The Model Release," *Videopro* 3 (November 1984): 67.
11. 8 Med. L. Rptr. 2366 (N.Y. Ct. App. 1982).
12. AFTRA covers vocalists, actors, announcers, narrators, and sound effects artists.
13. *Corliss v. E. W. Walker Co.*, 64 F. 280, 282-282 (C.C. Mass 1894) (No. 3,152).
14. 603 P.2d 425, 425 (Cal. 1979).
15. "Presley Publicity Right Not Inheritable," *Art & the Law* 5 (1980): 95.
16. 579 F.2d 215 (2d Cir. 1978).
17. 59 Misc. 2d 444 (1968).
18. *Namath v. Sports Illustrated*, 1 Med. L. Rptr. 1843, 1843 (N.Y. App. Div. 1975).
19. 1 Med. L. Rptr. 1784 (N.Y. App. Div. 1962).
20. *Nonprint Media and the Copyright Law: An Educator's Responsibilities and Rights* (N.p.: Anne Arundel County Public Schools, 1984), unpaged.
21. Gary H. Becker, *The Copyright Game* (Sanford, FL: Becker, 1983), p. 5.
22. Letter, 29 May 1985.
23. 203 U.S.P.Q. 484 (S.D.N.Y. 1978).
24. 207 U.S.P.Q. 97, 99 (2d Cir. 1980).
25. 208 U.S.P.Q. 580, 583-584 (S.D.N.Y. 1980).

26. 208 U.S.P.Q. 580, 583 (S.D.N.Y. 1980).
27. 215 U.S.P.Q. 289, 292 (2d Cir. 1982); see also, for example, *Walt Disney v. Air Pirates; Wainwright;* and *Dallas Cowboys Cheerleaders v. Scoreboard Posters,* 203 U.S.P.Q. 321 (5th Cir. 1979).
28. 215 U.S.P.Q. 289, 295 (2d Cir. 1982).
29. 572 F. Supp. 1186, 1189 (N.D. Ga. 1983).
30. 572 F. Supp. 1186, 1191-1192 (N.D. Ga. 1983).
31. 572 F. Supp. 1186, 1192 (N.D. Ga. 1983).
32. 572 F. Supp. 1186, 1195 (N.D. Ga. 1983); but this argument did not hold up in *Sony!*
33. 244 U.S.P.Q. 131, 133 (11th Cir. 1984).
34. 37 F. 202, 202 (S.D.N.Y. 1888).
35. Stephen A. Spataro, "Photography," in *Copyright: Selected Practical Approaches to Protection and Enforcement,* p. 165.
36. *Photography: What's the Law?* 2nd ed. (New York: Crown Publishers, 1979), p. 119.
37. Jack Manning, "Leisure/Camera View: An Inside Look at Picture Agencies and Stock Houses," *New York Times,* 3 July 1977, pp. 25; 27.
38. Martha H. Smith, letter, 29 May 1985.
39. For a further discussion of using image libraries see, for example, William Tucker, "Using Image Libraries," *E & I TV* 17 (November 1985): 32-33; 36.
40. "Tracking Down the Perfect Picture: Reflections of an Author of Informational Books," *CBC Features* 40 (1985-1986): unpaged.
41. Letter, 29 May 1985.
42. Gertz, Van Petten, and Van Petten, p. 9.

CHAPTER 13:

MUSIC, MUSIC, MUSIC

You have the literary property rights and fantastic visuals for your production. Now, you want to enhance your production with music. Or, maybe, your friend has a rock band and asks you to produce the band's first music-video. Since music is a copyrightable commodity, you must obtain the necessary authorizations.

SYNCHRONIZATION LICENSES

You simply cannot take a recorded song and transfer it to your background track—not even if you record it with your own orchestra. Sound tracks require at least three basic rights: (a) the right to publicly perform the music on the soundtrack; (b) the right to record the music in synchronization with the visuals; and (c) the right to distribute the music. Productions requesting these music rights usually fall into one of four production categories: (a) full-length theatrical film (for example, *Saturday Night Fever*, *Flashdance*, and *Fame*); (b) nonprofit, educational, religious, or cultural productions (for example, a Black History Month production might want to include recitals by Black poets); (c) TV commercials (for example, Diamond Crystal Salt used "Chitty, Chitty, Bang, Bang"); and (d) TV features and series. [1]

A **synchronization license** (or **sync license**) allows you "to record music in synchronism or timed-relation with a picture in the form of film, slidefilm [*sic*], filmstrip, videotape, video cassette [*sic*], etc." [2] A sync license is generally a non-exclusive license granted by the copyright owner of a musical composition to (a) record and re-record such musical composition in timed relation (that is, synchronization) with a series of visual images; (b) fix the musical composition as part of the completed work; and (c) make copies of the completed work. It may be granted for a limited term or in perpetuity. [3]

As noted in Chapter 11, ASCAP, BMI, and SESAC handle the small performing rights for almost all musical compositions. In 1948, a district court prohibited ASCAP-motion picture exhibitor agreements implying sync rights and performing rights are independent rights. [4] Thus, the producer usually must negotiate sync rights for music in the ASCAP catalog with the copyright proprietors. BMI and SESAC do handle some sync rights for their members.

Sync licenses for many professional and industrial productions are handled by The Harry Fox Agency. [5] It offers a non-theatrical sync license for schools and industry, churches and civic centers, and similar organizations. So, if you are producing a show on "no smoking" or one for all automobile dealers associated with your company or one for university student recruitment, this is the license you want.

Different factors affect the cost. Is it a profit or nonprofit production? Will your production be shown once or many times? How many minutes will the music be used? Will the use be visual vocal (i.e., you see the singer), visual instrumental, background vocal, or background instrumental? Is the production part of a series? Who is the intended audience? Will it be shown only in the U.S. or internationally? As a broadcast or a transmission? For one year or many? The cost ranges from several hundred to thousands of dollars. [6] The Ford Motor Company reportedly paid $100,000 to use "Help!" for one year. [7] And one composer, upon hearing his music as background to a radio commercial, only calmed down when his manager told him he was being paid $50,000 a year for the rights. [8]

SYNC LICENSE V. COMPULSORY LICENSE

Sync licenses are NOT governed by copyright law or other legislation, but by "voluntary" industry standards and practices—practices acknowledged by the courts in cases such as *Jerome v. Twentieth Century Fox Film Corp.* (over "Sweet Rosie O'Grady"), *Encore Music v. London Film Productions* (over "Managua Nicaragua"), and *Foreign & Domestic Music Corp. v. Licht* (over four songs used in the *Ecstasy* soundtrack). They are often confused with the compulsory license for making and distributing phonorecords of nondramatic musical compositions (in sheet music form) granted in Section 115. [9]

Section 115 retained—with substantial changes—the compulsory (or mechanical) license for making phonorecords of copyrighted nondramatic musical compositions first granted under the 1909 Act. The 1909 Act granted copyright owners of a musical composition the exclusive right to make or license the first recording. After that, others could make "similar use" of the work.

The compulsory license becomes available as soon as the music's copyright owner distributes phonorecords to the United States public. (This distribution must be authorized by the music's copyright owner). But, it applies only to making phonorecords for distribution to the public for private use. Background music systems such as Muzak must obtain the copyright owner's permission. Also excluded from this license is the unauthorized duplication of a musical sound recording originally developed and produced by another.

You can make a new arrangement of the work as long as the basic melody or fundamental character of the work is not changed. The new arrangement may not be copyrighted without the copyright owner's authorization.

You must notify the copyright owner, before or within thirty days after the phonorecords have been made, of your intent to use the material. The Copyright Office does not provide printed forms for this purpose. The "Notice of Intention" must be clearly headed "Notice of Intention to Obtain a Compulsory License for Making and Distributing Phonorecords." It must include information such as the full legal name and business address of the person or entity intending to obtain the license; whether the person or entity is a corporation, partnership, individual proprietorship, etc.; the person or entity's fiscal year; the title of the nondramatic musical work involved; the intended format (for example, cassette, long-playing disk); expected date of initial distribution; and the recording artists or group involved. If the copyright owner's identity and address are known, the Notice should be sent to the owner by certified or registered mail. No notice needs to be filed in the Copyright Office. If the copyright owner(s) and address are unknown, the Notice is sent to the Copyright Office with a $6.00 filing fee (an additional $4.00 will provide a Certificate of Filing upon request). [10] You cannot distribute any phonorecords before this notice. Failure to file the notice opens you to claims of copyright infringement.

The music's copyright owner must be identified in the Copyright Office's or other public record in order to receive royalties from the compulsory license. The royalty rate is established by the law at 2 3/4 cents per composition or 1/2 cent per minute or fraction of playing time, whichever is larger. Many record producers negotiate a lower rate. The Harry Fox Agency often handles these licenses. [11]

Once granted to one party, the compulsory license cannot be denied to others. Sync licenses, on the other hand, can be denied since they are granted solely at the copyright owner's discretion.

MASTER AND ADAPTATION RIGHTS

If you want to re-record from a phonorecord, tape recording, or film clip, you must obtain a **master rights license** in addition to the sync license. A master rights license is usually granted by the record company. Again, this can be expensive because of union contracts requiring the payment of "reuse fees" (that is, musicians, vocalists, etc. are paid when the recording is used in a new medium). As of 1983, the American Federation of Musicians' (AFM) agreement called for reuse fees of approximately $150 per musician. "Thus, a master recording embodying the performance of a 50 piece orchestra will be more expensive to use than a master recording embodying the performance of a few musicians." [12]

As mentioned earlier, sound tracks also require a performance license. The exact nature of the performing rights (small or grand) depends upon how the musical composition will be used. If your production is strictly for home use, you may not need the performance license. [13] But, better safe than sorry—do not pass up the performance license while negotiating the other licenses. (Producers usually try to obtain the sync and performing rights simultaneously.)

If you decide to alter or adapt the musical composition in any way, you also need to negotiate **adaptation rights**. Basically "these rights involve the alteration or adaptation of musical compositions by way of arrangement, parody, comedic use, lyric change, translation, etc." These rights can be difficult to obtain because "specific permission, directly from the copyright owner, may be required before broadcast or release. Some copyright owners, while open to the use of their material as it was originally written, will not grant permission for any adaptations." [14]

Since each musical composition has its own unique set of legal and business issues, there is no set clearance pattern. For example, a top forty song may not be available for other media applications. Unauthorized use of the song could result in a lawsuit delaying your production's exhibition until the song is removed and imposing financial penalties. [15]

OTHER USABLE MUSIC

Three alternate sources for music are public domain, specially composed, and production music libraries.

Some producers pride themselves on using classical music. "After all," they say, "it is in the public domain." Unfortunately, this is not quite true. The music itself may be in the public domain, but the particular arrangement used and the orchestra's rendition may be copyrighted (see Chapter 15 for a discussion of public domain materials).

114

You can hire a composer to create a sound track for you.   If the sound track is specially composed by a composer you hired, it is a work for hire.   This means you do not need a sync license since you own the whole copyright in the music.

John Williams may be too expensive, but many university music departments teach composition.   You might be able to work out an arrangement with either a faculty member or a graduate student as well as the university orchestra.   If you hire musicians, be sure to check the AFM's Minimum Basic Agreement for fees.   For example, the basic session rate for a three-hour nonclassical recording session was $196.41 as of December 1, 1985.

Sound effect and production music libraries (also known as cleared music libraries) require the payment of clearance fees in addition to the purchase of the library's album(s).   Usually there are two rate categories: (a) non-broadcast, which includes industrial and educational productions, and (b) broadcast, which includes network, cable, and syndicated TV and radio.   As with other production elements, negotiate the rates.

Depending upon the particular library, you may find up to four ways to pay for clearances.   For example, Thomas J. Valentino, Inc. quoted the following clearance fees in its 1985 brochure:

1.   **"Needle drop"** (or **"per use"**) rates ranged from $40-50 depending upon the rate category involved.   In the case of TV and radio spot commercials, the range was $50-250 depending on local, regional, or national use.   (Large metropolitan areas such as New York, Los Angeles, Chicago, and Dallas/Fort Worth were considered regional.) If you multiply the length of the selection used by the number of times it is used in the production, you find that the fee quickly adds up.   For example, a two-minute long selection used five times during a production translates into a $200-250 fee depending on the rate category.

2.   **"Unlimited use"** rates, based on the length of the production, found non-broadcast production varying from $150 for fifteen minutes to $250 for sixty minutes.   (Broadcast: $400/thirty minutes-$900/ninety minutes)

115

3. **"Annual agreement"** fees (or **"annual blanket licenses"**) included thirty free albums and ran $1,200 for non-broadcast and $1,500 for broadcast.

4. **"Single theme licenses"** granting the unlimited use of one specific theme was offered for an annual one time license of $500.

The National Federation of Local Cable Programmers offers the DeWolf Music Library as a service to its members. The library ranges from classical to electronic pieces. An annual fee of $178 secures synchronization rights to nine records of choice. [16]

One-price production music libraries, or buy-out libraries, are another alternative. "Once you buy the album(s), you own all rights except one: the right to manufacture and sell that album . . . . [Y]ou needn't pay royalties, nor file any reports on usage. You pay only once. [*sic*] and you pay only one fee." [17] Since your one-time purchase price includes all the production rights you need, these albums are slightly more expensive than those requiring additional fees. Prices can range from $80 to $250. Some buy-out libraries charge additional fees for broadcast rights, so check the fine print.

A Producer's Guide to Music Clearance warned that "if you are a union signatory, or are producing for a union signatory company, be sure to use caution as some production music may not comply with union requirements." As Sam Stalos noted in his December 1984 *AV Video* editorial: "The recording of library music is not sanctioned by the musicians' union, which is why a lot of the music is recorded abroad. The rest is recorded in non-union sessions . . . ." [18]

Of course, you also might ask yourself if music is really necessary for your production. It is often hard to find music geared to educational needs. You risk the audience listening to the music and not the narration. And, especially in cases of pop music, it may date your production.

MUSIC VIDEOS

The current trend toward music videos highlights some of the problems involved in combining music and visuals into one production. For example, videodiscs do not fit the Section 101 definitions for either an audiovisual work or sound recording. So which copyright registration form do you use to register your videodisc—Form PA for works of the performing arts or Form SR for sound recordings? At first glance, videodiscs seem to fit the motion picture definition,[19] so you would use Form PA.

Since contractual standards are in a state of flux until the true market potential has been established, the specifics of negotiating music videos varies between record companies. *Lindey on Entertainment, Publishing and the Arts* identified seven major negotiation points for music video producers:

- the right to produce the video;

- ownership of the finished video;

- financing and recouping production costs;

- the right to "exploit" the video for promotional and commercial uses;

- distributing any income between the royalty artists, producers, etc.;

- synchronization and performing rights; and,

- master recording rights. [20]

Shemel and Krasilovsky added two points:

- the right to make copies of the musical composition; and,

- the right to distribute copies to the public. [21]

Broadcast fees may start at $1,000. The exclusive, first right to exhibit a video — like MTV's right to Michael Jackson's "Thriller"

117

documentary and the fourteen minute promotional video made from it—may run as high as $250,000.   Annual or semi-annual licenses for nightclub showings of videos may start at $5 per video per month as opposed to $75 per video per month on a nonsubscription basis. [22]

Platinum Record Company v. Lucasfilm, which focused on master recording rights and videodiscs, perhaps illustrates the problems involved.   Chess Janus Records, Platinum's predecessor, gave Lucasfilm the right to use master recordings (or matrixes) of four popular songs for the *American Graffiti* sound track ("Almost Grown," "Johnnie B. Goode," "Book of Love," and "Goodnight Sweetheart").   The conditions for use included the "right to record, dub and synchronize" with the motion picture and trailers "and to exhibit, distribute, exploit, market and perform said motion picture, its air, screen and television trailers, perpetually throughout the world by any means or methods now or hereafter known." [23]

Universal released the film which was a success and shown on cable, network, and local TV.   MCA (a Universal affiliate) released the film for sale and rental to the public in videocassette and videodisc formats.   Platinum sued for breach of contract because videodiscs were not listed as a potential use of the film.   The court found the contract's language broad, completely unambiguous, and precluding the need for an exhaustive list of specific potential uses of the film.   The videocassettes and videodiscs were merely additional means of exhibition.   Thus, Lucasfilm's motion for a summary judgment was granted.

FAIR USE

As with visuals, if you want to use music in your production, you probably will be outside the scope of fair use.   Fair use guidelines for educational uses of music (see Appendix C) were negotiated by the concerned parties and transmitted to Congress on April 30, 1976.   They were subsequently included in House Report 94-1476.

There seems to be some agreement that a one time use of a recorded song while teaching a unit on synchronizing audio and visuals in a media production class is fair use. [24] The inclusion of a few lines of lyrics in an article has been deemed fair use (e.g., *Karll v. Curtis Publishing Company* [25]). But, even copying eight notes of music may be an infringement (*Fisher v. Dillingham* [26]). Parodies sometimes have been considered fair use, as with *Mad*'s parodies of song lyrics. [27] But Jack Benny's parody of *Gaslight* was considered an infringement. [28]

REFERENCES

1. Sidney Shemel and M. William Krasilovsky, *This Business of Music*, 5th ed. (New York: Billboard Publications, 1985), p. 95.
2. The Harry Fox Agency, Request for Non-Theatric Quotation (mimeographed form).
3. *Lindey on Entertainment, Publishing and the Arts*, 2nd ed., 3 vols. (New York: Clark Boardman, 1984), 2A:1522.237.
4. *Alden-Rochelle, Inc. v. ASCAP*, 80 F. Supp. 888 (S.D.N.Y. 1948).
5. For a list of rights and permissions agencies see Jerome K. Miller's *The Copyright Directory, Vol. I: General Information*, Chapter 3.
6. Henry Marks, Harry Fox Agency, Phone conversation, 12 July 1985; Request for Non-Theatric Quotation; and Edward R. Hearn, "Legal Aspects of Video Productions," *Video Systems* (August 1987): 59.
7. "Business Notes: A Thriller of a Deal," *Time* 126 (26 August 1985): 46.
8. "Personal Glimpses," *Reader's Digest* 127 (September 1985): 130.
9. *Jerome*, 70 U.S.P.Q. 349 (S.D.N.Y. 1946), *aff'd per curiam*, 76 U.S.P.Q. 246 (2d Cir. 1948); *Encore Music*, 89 U.S.P.Q. 501 (S.D.N.Y. 1951); *Foreign & Domestic Music*, 93 U.S.P.Q. 272 (2d Cir. 1952); and Section 115.
10. For a full description of the procedure, see 37 C.F.R. §201.18 (1986).
11. *Senate*, pp. 88-94; *House*, pp. 107-111; U.S., Congress, House, Committee of Conference, *General Revision of the Copyright*

Law, Title 17 of the United States Code, H. Rept. No. 94-1733, 94th Cong., 2d sess., 1976, p. 77.

12. Gertz, Van Petten, and Van Petten, p. 19.
13. Alan Bomser, Mitchell Bernstein, and Jay Lewin, "Legal Problems Re: Music in Video Recordings of Motion Pictures," in *Legal and Business Aspects of the Music Industry: Music, Videocassettes, and Records* (New York: Practising Law Institute, 1980), p. 636; *A Producer's Guide to Music Clearance* (Los Angeles: Clearing House, Ltd., 1985), unpaged.
14. *A Producer's Guide*, unpaged.
15. *A Producer's Guide*, unpaged.
16. Undated letter to Access Producers.
17. Sam Stalos, "The Band in the Background," *AV Video* 6 (December 1984): 46-47.
18. *A Producer's Guide*, unpaged; "Getting Away with It," p. 11. For in-depth looks at production music libraries see, for example, Bill Milbrodt, "Concerning Sound Tracks," *E & I TV* 17 (November 1985): 42-43; 54; and Stalos, "The Band in the Background," pp. 42-48. For a list of production music libraries see, for example, Miller, *The Copyright Directory*, Chapter 5.
19. Rena B. Denham, "The Problem of Musical Videodiscs: The Need for Performance Rights in Sound Recordings," *University of San Francisco Law Review* 16 (Fall 1981): 135.
20. 2A:1522.5.
21. p. 77.
22. Shemel and Krasilvosky, p. 76.
23. 566 F. Supp. 226, 227 (D. N.J. 1983).
24. For example, Charles L. Gary, letter, 12 June 1985; Henry Marks, 12 July 1985.
25. 51 U.S.P.Q. 50 (E.D. Wis. 1941).
26. 298 F. 145 (S.D.N.Y. 1924).
27. *Berlin v. E. C. Publications*, 141 U.S.P.Q. 1 (2d Cir. 1964).
28. *Loew's Inc. v. CBS*, 116 U.S.P.Q. 479 (1958).

CHAPTER 14:

PRINTED MATERIALS

Chances are you will want to develop some type of written manual—for students, instructors, or both—to accompany your audiovisual production. Or, perhaps, you must produce a course outline or guide. What copyrighted material, if any, may you include without the copyright owner's permission? The only way you could include copyrighted materials without authorization is under the doctrine of fair use.

FAIR USE

Fair use covers areas such as review and criticism—"Criticism is an important and proper exercise of fair use . . ." [1]—and incidental usage like the inclusion of a few lines of lyrics in an article. [2] Reproducing the entire text of a copyrighted article or chapter or musical composition would probably be beyond fair use. For example, the Kansas State Department of Education asked the Kansas Attorney General if its music teachers were allowed to duplicate copyrighted music for the judges' use at a state festival. The Kansas Attorney General replied that despite its nonprofit educational purpose, such copying was not permitted under Section 107's definition of fair use because

1) It does not constitute duplication for the purpose of criticizing or commenting on the copyrighted works

themselves; 2) even if regarded as being for the purpose of comment or criticism, duplication of an entire score exceeds the permissible amount which may fairly be reproduced as legitimately necessary for critical review; and 3) such duplication is intended primarily as a substitute for purchasing the original works. [3]

As noted in Chapter 5, court cases abound in this area. Consider these three example:

In *Association of American Medical Colleges v. Mikaelian*, the court said Mikaelian's MCAT "cram course" was not "teaching" in the generally understood sense. Also, since the enrollees paid to attend, there was no free, public dissemination of information. Thus, the court found Mikaelian's copying of the MCAT test questions did not fall under fair use. [4]

Rubin v. Boston Magazine Co. focused on Isaac Michael Rubin's "love scale" of twenty-six questions to help elicit feelings about others included in his copyrighted dissertation. He used the scale in several copyrighted works and even denied *Reader's Digest* permission to reproduce the scale. *Boston* (a magazine) published an article on love and included the scale—without permission. The court decided *Boston's* use of the scale was a commercial one and affected the scale's potential market. Fair use thus did not apply. (The district court awarded Rubin $7500.) [5]

Harper & Row v. Nation Enterprises found Harper & Row and the Readers Digest Association suing the publishers of *The Nation* for copyright infringement, conversion, and interference with contract. Victor Navasky, *The Nation's* editor, received an unauthorized draft of former President Gerald R. Ford's memoirs. These were soon to be published by Harper & Row with special prepublication rights to *Time*. Navasky thought the section on Ford's pardon of Nixon "hot news," so he rushed putting together an article quoting and paraphrasing sections of the book draft.

The Nation claimed fair use because it was "news." The district court disagreed. The article (1) was published for profit; (2) infringed a work shortly to be published; (3) took the heart of the book (*Time* had been willing to pay $25,000 for the Nixon pardon material.); and (4) caused the *Time* agreement to fall through, thus diminishing its value. The court awarded Harper & Row $12,500 in damages for *Time*'s non-performance and various other amounts of profits.

On appeal, the Second Circuit reversed the decision. The majority held that *The Nation*'s article was a news story and that the verbatim copying and paraphrasing were of mainly uncopyrightable material. The majority rejected the lower court's fair use analysis. The dissenting opinion maintained: "This Court has acknowledged that verbatim copying of a factual work is actionable as copyright infringement . . . . Paraphrasing, which is what took place here, is the equivalent of copying for purposes of the copyright laws." [6]

The Supreme Court reversed (6-3) the Second Circuit's decision. According to the Supreme Court, the question is "to what extent the 'fair use' provision . . . sanctions the unauthorized use of quotations from a public figure's unpublished manuscript." [7] Noting *Iowa State* and *Roy Export* (both discussed in previous chapters), the Court confirmed that newsworthiness does not justify copying. Turning to fair use, the Court agreed with the district court's analysis. Referring to *Time*'s cancellation and refusal to pay $12,500, the Court remarked: "Rarely will a case of copyright infringement present such clear cut evidence of actual damages." [8] The Supreme Court, therefore, found the district court had properly awarded actual damages and accounting of profits.

As discussed in Chapter 5, fair use in education, especially the guidelines, is aimed primarily at the classroom teacher. The print guidelines, for example, deal with multiple copies for classroom use or for the teacher's private use. Nowhere in fair use or its related guidelines is semester-to-semester use permitted. Fair use is a temporary measure. This excludes from fair use most articles reproduced for "class reading" packages. These "readings" are actually anthologies. They formed the basis for the lawsuit against New York University coordinated by the Association of American Publishers. (The lawsuit was settled out of court. NYU promised to adhere to the fair use guidelines.)

Continued use of an item requires permission from the copyright owner. Sometimes that permission is already granted near the copyright notice. For example:

Copyrighted material from *TechTrends* may be reproduced for noncommercial purposes provided full credit acknowledgments and a copyright notice appear on the reproduction. Other requests for reprinting should be addressed to AECT [Association for Educational Communications and Technology] Permissions.

or

All materials in this journal subject to copyright by ALA [American Library Association] may be photocopied for the noncommercial purpose of educational or scientific advancement.

But, if you plan to market your product—even for educational purposes—you probably are beyond the bounds of such blanket grants of permission to copy. You need the copyright owner's permission. In some cases, permission for copies for meetings, presentations, clients, workshops, and some classroom uses may be obtained through agencies such as the Copyright Clearance Center (see Appendix A for address). In other words, permission must be obtained directly from the copyright owner.

Sheet music presents similar problems; for example, copying out-of-print compositions, desiring to rearrange a composition, and reproducing "words-only" sheets or overhead transparencies for sing-alongs require authorization. The Music Publisher's Association of the USA prepared two forms to help simplify the permissions process: Inquiry Form on Out-of-Print Copyrighted Music (reproduced in Appendix B1) and Request for Permission to Arrange (reproduced in Appendix B2). Letter size (8 1/2" x 11") copies of these forms are available from the Music Educators National Conference (MENC; see Appendix A for the address). [9]

One of the better known cases involving the duplication of sheet music is *F.E.L. Publications v. Catholic Bishop of Chicago.*

F.E.L. Publications, a music publisher which publishes and markets hymnals to Roman Catholic parishes, brought action against the Catholic Bishop of Chicago (an Illinois corporation owning all the Catholic parish property in the archdiocese of Chicago) for copyright infringement, Lanham Act violations, and unfair competition.

The Roman Catholic Church has no national hymnal, so some parishes prepare custom-made hymnals to satisfy local needs. Prior to 1972, F.E.L. licensed Catholic parishes the right to copy songs at two cents per song per copy. When it perceived widespread infringement, F.E.L. instituted an Annual Copyright License in 1972 permitting parishes to copy F.E.L. songs in unlimited quantities for 1 year for $100. Copies were to be destroyed when the license terminated. F.E.L. also provided other low-cost arrangements. When it realized the license did not discourage illegal copying, F.E.L. filed suit under the 1909 Act. As a result, millions of "uncleared" hymnals were removed from Roman Catholic churches in the U.S. [10]

The district court held that F.E.L.'s copyright claim *barred* because the license was illegally used to extend copyright over exempt performances of copyrighted music and was a violation of the Sherman Act. It also dismissed the Lanham Act charge because of a jurisdictional problem. Finally, it dismissed the state claim because it declined the jurisdiction. [11]

The Seventh Circuit found this summary judgment in error. According to the Seventh Circuit, a copyright owner's exclusive rights include printing, publishing, copying, and performing (under 1909 Act). The copyright owner cannot prevent not-for-profit performances of works, nor exact a fee for it. Singing hymns at religious services is a not-for-profit performance which F.E.L. cannot prevent. But, F.E.L. can prevent the copying or publishing of its works—even if churches only intend a not-for-profit performance. Distributing the copies needs the copyright owner's permission. Performing music at not-for-profit religious services implies from memory or from legal copies. "Neither the religious element nor the non-profit element of a performance will protect illegal copying or publishing." [12]

On further appeal, the Seven Circuit affirmed the $190,400 for F.E.L.'s copyright infringement claim but vacated the $3 million in damages and later denied F.E.L.'s petition for rehearing concerning the reversal of the jury's $3 million award. Though the U.S. Supreme Court refused to hear the case, the district court awarded F.E.L. the largest attorneys' fees award ever made in a U.S. copyright infringement case: $135,696.52. [13] F.E.L. now has a suit in the federal appellate court, for 8 million dollars, charging the Catholic Bishop with leading a national boycott of F.E.L. music. So stay tuned for future installments!

TEACHER VERSUS TEACHER

A teacher would never sue another teacher for copyright infringement. Right? Wrong! Eloise Toby Marcus sued Shirley Rowley and the San Diego Unified School District for copyright infringement. Marcus, a public school teacher, owned a registered copyright to a booklet on cake decorating. Rowley, also a public school teacher, incorporated a substantial portion of this copyrighted work in a booklet she prepared for her classes. The district court dismissed the action on the grounds that Rowley's copying was fair use. The Ninth Circuit disagreed—and so reversed the decision.

How did this lawsuit originate? Between 1972 and 1974, Marcus taught home economics for the San Diego Unified School District. Shortly after leaving the district, she wrote a booklet, *Cake Decorating Made Easy*, which was thirty-five pages long (twenty-nine original pages, six with permission of authors). She only sold the booklet to her adult education classes with a full copyright notice in each booklet.

Rowley taught food service career classes for San Diego Unified. She took Marcus's course in 1975 and bought the booklet. The following summer, she prepared an activity package, *Cake Decorating Learning Activity Package*, for use in her classes. Fifteen copies were kept in a file for student use. No charge was made for using the activity package. This package included eleven pages from Marcus and four pages from other authors Marcus had used with permission. No credit was given Marcus.

Marcus learned of Rowley's package when a student accused Marcus of plagiarizing Rowley's work! The student's son had obtained Rowley's package from class and shown it to his parent who then thought Marcus had copied it.

The court said it did not matter whether the case was under the 1909 or the 1976 Act because it "would not affect the outcome of this case since its resolution turns entirely on the application of the doctrine of fair use." [14] And since Section 107 is simply a restatement of judicial doctrine, those factors can be used in analyzing the applicability of fair use to this case.

The court said that even though Rowley's package was for nonprofit educational purposes and at no charge, it "does not automatically compel a finding of fair use." [15] Looking at *MacMillan v. King*, the court noted that being a teacher does not matter: "[A] finding that the alleged infringers copied the material to use it for the same intrinsic purpose for which the copyright owner intended it to be used is strong indicia of no fair use." [16] Here, both booklets were prepared to teach cake decorating, so it weighs against a finding of fair use. Also, Rowley did not secure permission or even attempt to; nor did she credit Marcus. Again, this weighs against a finding of fair use.

Turning to the question of the nature of the copyrighted work, the court focused on whether the work was informational or creative since informational works have a greater fair use scope. The court found that though some basic facts were included in the booklet, it basically reflected Marcus's own creative hints based on experience. "Thus, on balance, it does not appear that analysis of this factor is of any real assistance in reaching a conclusion as to applicability of fair use." [17]

The third fair use criteria, amount and substantiality of portion used, was then applied. Since "wholesale copying of copyrighted material precludes application of the fair use doctrine" and Rowley's was "both substantial quantitative and qualitative copying," fair use does not apply here. [18]

In terms of the effect upon the potential market, "the mere absence of measurable pecuniary damage does not require a finding of fair use." [19]

Thus, after analyzing the factors, the court found no fair use. Its "conclusion is in harmony with the Congressional guidelines which ... merit consideration with respect to the issue of fair use in an educational context." While the guidelines do not control the court, "they are instructive on the issue of fair use in the context of the case." [20] The court found Rowley's use did not meet the guidelines. Thus, the court found for Marcus.

Looking at the court cases discussed here and in Chapter 5, it readily becomes apparent that despite Section 107's inclusion of teaching as an example of fair use, educational purposes and fair use are not synonymous terms. To include printed materials in your production, play it safe—obtain the copyright owner's permission.

REFERENCES

1. *Loew's Inc. v. CBS*, 105 U.S.P.Q. 302, 310 (S.D. Cal. 1955).
2. See, for example, *Karll v. Curtis Publishing Company*, 51 U.S.P.Q. 50 (E.D. Wis. 1941).
3. Schools—State Music Festivals—Duplication of Copyrighted Works, 15 Ops. Kan. Atty. Gen. 202 (1981).
4. 571 F. Supp. 144 (E.D. Pa. 1983).
5. 209 U.S.P.Q. 1073 (1st Cir. 1981).
6. 220 U.S.P.Q. 321, 334 (2d Cir. 1983).
7. 225 U.S.P.Q. 1073, 1073 (1985).
8. 225 U.S.P.Q. 1073, 1083 (1985).
9. For an in-depth discussion of this problem, especially as it affects religious organizations, see Martha A. Bentley, *Copyright: Insights for the Christian Musician* (Chadron, NE: Jaybee Enterprises, 1980).
10. Jerome K. Miller to Esther R. Sinofsky, 20 August 1987.
11. 210 U.S.P.Q. 403 (N.D. Ill. 1981).
12. 214 U.S.P.Q. 409, 411 (7th Cir. 1982).
13. 225 U.S.P.Q. 278 (7th Cir. 1985); *History of the Litigation*, (F.E.L. Publications, Ltd., mimeograph, n.d.).
14. 217 U.S.P.Q. 691, 693 (9th Cir. 1983).
15. 217 U.S.P.Q. 691, 694.
16. 217 U.S.P.Q. 691, 695.
17. 217 U.S.P.Q. 691, 695.
18. 217 U.S.P.Q. 691, 695-696.
19. 217 U.S.P.Q. 691, 696-697.
20. 217 U.S.P.Q. 691, 697.

CHAPTER 15:

PUBLIC DOMAIN MATERIALS

As briefly mentioned in previous chapters, works in the public domain represent one of the cheapest sources for production materials. "Television film scores and advertising jingles and announcements frequently use public domain music . . . to avoid high synchronization fees and to have full freedom to adapt to any form." [1]

Basically, public domain refers to materials that are no longer or never have been under copyright protection. Such works normally fall into one of four categories:

1. Works never copyrighted.

2. Uncopyrightable works.

3. Works whose copyright has expired.

4. Works for which no one can really claim authorship.

A lack of copyright notice does not automatically place a work in the public domain. Section 405 addresses this issue. It makes clear that "the outright omission of a copyright notice does not automatically forfeit protection and throw the work into the public domain." [2] However, if no effort to correct the error or register the work is made, the work enters the public domain after five years.

Section 405 also discusses the effect of the omission of a copyright notice on an innocent infringer. In other words, if a person innocently infringes a copyright because the copyright notice was omitted, the person is not liable for actual or statutory damages for infringements committed before notification of the work's registered status.

> The general postulates underlying the provision are that a person acting in good faith and with no reason to think otherwise should ordinarily be able to assume that a work is in the public domain if there is no notice on an authorized copy or phonorecord and that, if he relies on this assumption, he should be shielded from unreasonable liability. [3]

The court decides if the copyright owner receives any of the innocent infringer's profits from the "before notification" period, whether the material may still be used and, if so, whether a license fee must be paid the copyright owners (see Circular R22 reproduced in Appendix D11 for a summary of this point).

Differences between foreign and U.S. copyright laws also create difficulties in determining the status of works. For example, Bram Stoker's *Dracula* has always been in the public domain in the U.S. because it failed to comply with the 1897 deposit requirements. However, in England and other Berne Convention countries it only entered the public domain in April 1962. [4] And, though copyright has expired in works more than seventy-five years old, derivative works may still be copyrighted.

WORKS NEVER COPYRIGHTED

If a work never has been copyrighted, it enters the public domain. For example, Peter Max, a famous illustrator, used a photograph of Mick Jagger in one of his collage-type paintings. Since the photograph had been published without a copyright notice before January 1, 1978, the court held the photograph was in the public domain. [5]

131

In *Excel Promotions Corp. v. Babylon Beacon, Inc.*, both parties published weekly newspapers. Excel Promotions claimed Babylon Beacon infringed its copyright in certain advertisements. However, the court agreed that the ads fell under the "work made for hire" category making the advertisers the owners. Furthermore, since Excel Promotions' order form concerned the insertion of ads, not the transfer of copyrights, the advertisers remained the advertisement's copyright owners. So Excel Promotions could not copyright the advertisements and, thus, Babylon Beacon could not be liable for infringing a non-existent copyright. However, since a copyright notice did not appear on the advertisements and the advertisers were not set forth as the copyright owners, the advertisements entered the public domain. [6]

UNCOPYRIGHTABLE WORKS

The classic example is *Baker v. Selden*. Selden sued Baker for infringing the blank forms included in his *Selden's Condensed Ledger, or Bookkeeping Simplified.* The Supreme Court found that "blank accountbooks are not the subject of copyright." [7] Thus, it dismissed the charge against Baker. Recent cases have modified *Baker v. Selden.* The Copyright Office circular on blank forms (see Appendix D2) was revised to reflect these changes.

WORKS WHOSE COPYRIGHT HAS EXPIRED

The problem of derivative works tends to confuse the issues in this category. For example, what happens when the derivative work enters the public domain, but the original work is still copyrighted? Or, what if the derivative work enters the public domain, but the original work is protected by common law copyright? *Filmvideo Releasing Corp. v. Hastings, Cyril Russell v. Daniel A. Price*, and *Classic Film Museum v. Warner Brothers* (see Chapter 4 for a discussion of these cases) illustrate these problems.

WORKS FOR WHICH NO ONE
CAN CLAIM AUTHORSHIP

Folk songs (or folk-like songs) best exemplify this type of public domain work. Questions raised by works in this category include

[W]ho should get the money that would normally flow to the originator of a work such as "Tom Dooley"—Frank Proffitt, the "informant" [shared the song with folk-song collectors]? Frank Warner or Alan Lomax, the collectors? The Trio [The Kingston Trio], the popularizers? Somehow the public in whose domain the song may be? Or is "Tom Dooley" available for exploitation without permission or royalties? [8]

The entertainment industry itself adds to the problem. It wants to "receive permission" from someone. According to Oscar Brand,

"If I were to sing 'The Battle Hymn of the Republic' on a program, the 'music clearance' department would insist on knowing the name of some ... publisher ... willing to claim authorship .... This compounds the problems, by producing many copyrights to some folk songs." [9]

In other words, if you play the original public-domain song exactly as it originally appeared, you are safe. The slightest variation in arrangement can lead to the infringement of someone's copyrighted "new" version (cases are cited in the following section).

PUBLIC DOMAIN AND MUSICAL COMPOSITIONS

Sheet music over seventy-five years old is assumed to be in the public domain, especially since a transitional provision of the 1976 Act put nondramatic musical works copyrighted before July 1, 1909, in the public domain. A defective copyright notice placed "The

Caissons Go Rolling Along" in the public domain. However, "new" arrangements still may be protected by copyright.

There are several sources for checking the public domain status of a musical work, for example: Lincoln Center Library of the Performing Arts; The Harry Fox Agency; and "The Archive of Folk Culture" at the Library of Congress.

A sampling of the court cases further highlights the problems involved. In *N. Lindsay Norden v. Oliver Ditson Company*, the plaintiff tried to prevent the defendant from publishing Arkhangelsky's "O Light Divine," claiming it infringed his Arkhangelsky composition "O Gladsome Light." The plaintiff's work was an adaptation of public domain Russian music.

Looking first at whether the plaintiff's work was copyrightable, the court restated a basic copyright tenet: "to be the subject of a copyright [a composition] must have sufficient originality to make it a new work rather than a copy of the old with minor changes which any skilled musician might make. It must be the result of some original or creative work." [10] Comparing Norden's adaptation to this criterion, the court found the work not copyrightable. Thus, the defendant freely could use the work. [11]

In *Wihtol v. Wells*, Austries A. Wihtol charged that Kenneth H. Wells, an ordained minister, of infringing his copyrighted song "My God and I." (The same song later became the focus of *Wihtol v. Crow*, involving a music teacher. [12]) Though Wihtol's tune was based on an old Latvian, Russian, or Italian folksong in the public domain, the Seventh Circuit found that Wihtol added something creative and original to it. Thus, Wihtol's work was copyrightable. Since Wells' work was almost identical, it was an infringement. [13]

REFERENCES

1. Shemel and Krasilovsky, p. 250.
2. *House, p.* 146.
3. *House, p.* 148.
4. *Lugosi,* 603 P.2d 425, 427.
5. *Goldsmith v. Max,* Copy. L. Rep. (CCH) ¶25,248 (S.D.N.Y. 1981).
6. 207 U.S.P.Q. 616 (E.D.N.Y. 1979).
7. 101 U.S. 99, 107 (1879).
8. O. Wayne Coon, "Some Problems with Musical Public-domain Materials Under United States Copyright Law as Illustrated Mainly by the Recent Folk-song Revival," in *ASCAP Copyright Law Symposium* (New York: Columbia University Press, 1971), p. 191.
9. Cited in Coon, p. 197.
10. 28 U.S.P.Q. 183, 186 (D.Mass. 1936).
11. For a similar discussion of copyrightability of public domain works, see *Alfred Bell & Co. Ltd. v. Catalda Fine Arts, Inc.,* 90 U.S.P.Q. 153 (2d Cir. 1951).
12. 132 U.S.P.Q. 392 (S.D. Iowa 1961), *rev'd,* 135 U.S.P.Q. 385 (8th Cir. 1962).
13. 109 U.S.P.Q. 200 (7th Cir. 1956).

APPENDICES

TABLE OF CONTENTS

APPENDIX A:

ADDRESS AND TELEPHONE DIRECTORY

1. The Copyright Office

A.   Forms

> Information and Publications Section LM-455
> Copyright Office
> Library of Congress
> Washington, DC 20559
> 202/287-8700 (8:30 A.M. - 5:00 P.M. EST)
> 202/287-9100 (24 hour hotline for requesting registration forms)

B. Searches

> Reference and Bibliography Section LM-451
> Copyright Office
> Library of Congress
> Washington, DC 20559
> 202/287-6850

2. Title Registry

> Motion Picture Title Directory
> Motion Picture Association of America
> 1133 Avenue of the Americas
> New York, NY 10036
> 212/840-6161
> Contact: Dorothy Beer

3. Small Rights (Nondramatic Musical Performances)

A. American Society of Composers, Authors & Publishers (ASCAP)
One Lincoln Plaza
New York, NY 10023
212/595-3050

B. Broadcast Music, Inc. (BMI)
40 West 57th Street
New York, NY 10019
212/586-2000

C. SESAC, Inc.
10 Columbus Circle
New York, NY 10019
212/586-3450

4. Grand Rights (Dramatic/Dramatico-Musical Performances)

A. Music Theatre International
119 West 57th Street
New York, NY 10019
212/975-6841

B. Rodgers & Hammerstein Library
598 Madison Avenue
New York, NY 10022
212/486-7378

C. Samuel French, Inc.
1. East Coast
45 West 25th Street
New York, NY 10010
212/206-8990

2. West Coast (AK, AZ, CA, CO, HI, ID, MT, NV, NM, OR, UT, WA, WY. Except orders for musicals)
7623 Sunset Boulevard
Los Angeles, CA 90046
213/876-0570

D. Tams-Witmark Music Library, Inc.
757 Third Avenue
New York, NY 10017
212/688-2525

5. Clearinghouses

A. The Clearing House, Ltd.
6605 Hollywood Boulevard, Suite 200
Los Angeles, CA 90028
213/469-3186

B. Copyright Clearance Center, Inc.
27 Congress Street
Salem, MA 01970
617/744-3350

C. The Harry Fox Agency
110 East 59th Street
New York, NY 10022
212/751-1930

6. Guilds, Unions, and Associations (check telephone directory for chapters in your area)

A. American Federation of Musicians (AFM)
1. East Coast
1501 Broadway, Suite 600
New York, NY 10036
212/869-1330

2. West Coast
1777 Vine Street
Los Angeles, CA 90028
213/461-3441

B. American Federation of Television & Radio Artists (AFTRA)
1. East Coast
1350 Avenue of the Americas
New York, NY 10019
212/265-7700

2. West Coast
1717 North Highland Avenue
Los Angeles, CA 90028
213/461-8111

C. American Society of Magazine Photographers (ASMP)
1. East Coast
205 Lexington Avenue
New York, NY 10016
212/889-9144

2. West Coast
P.O. Box 480530
Los Angeles, CA 90048
213/466-9463

D. Music Educators National Conference (MENC)
1902 Association Drive
Reston, VA 22091
703/860-4000

E. Music Publishers' Association of the U.S. (MPA)
Third Floor
130 West 57th Street
New York, NY 10019
212/582-1122

F. National Federation of Local Cable Programmers (NFLCP)
906 Pennsylvania Avenue, SE
Washington, DC 20003
202/544-7272

G. National Music Publishers' Association, Inc. (NMPA)
110 East 59th Street
New York, NY 10022
212/751-1930

H. Screen Actors Guild (SAG)
7750 West Sunset Boulevard
Los Angeles, CA 90046
213/876-7411 (Contracts)

7. Copyright Consultants

   A. Brylawski, Cleary & Leeds
      224 East Capitol Street
      Washington, DC 20003
      202/547-1331

   B. Jerome K. Miller, President
      Copyright Information Services
      P.O. Box 1460
      Friday Harbor, WA 98250
      206/378-5128

APPENDIX B1:

INQUIRY FORM ON OUT-OF-PRINT
COPYRIGHTED MUSIC

INQUIRY FORM ON OUT-OF-PRINT COPYRIGHTED MUSIC

Prepared by: Music Publisher's Association of the United States, and
National Music Publishers' Association Inc.

INSTRUCTIONS

This form is to be prepared in duplicate. After completing the boxed section and signing both copies where indicated, forward them to the publisher who will complete the form and return it to you. If the publisher indicates a payment for the right you request, and if the conditions are agreeable to you, remit the amount to the publisher together with the original copy, which he will have signed, whereupon the agreement will be completed.

To:_____
       (Name of Publisher)

Address:_____

_____

I (We) wish to procure _____ copies of your copyrighted publication:

_____

       (Title)   (Arrangement)

by:_____

If it is in print:
Please indicate the price per copy here _____

If it is out of print:
A) Do you have plans to reprint it? _____ If so, when? _____

    At what price per copy? _____

B) If there are no plans for reprinting I (we) request your permission to have a non-exclusive right to reproduce by photocopy_____ copies for use by my (our)

(students, members, congregation, etc.)

145

As consideration for your permission to do so, I (we) will pay you in advance of making the copies_____per copy, totalling $_____.

The copies will be identical to your publication including the copyright notice. The following will be legibly included on the first page of each copy of our reproduction:

> "This reproduction is made with the express consent
> of _____
> (copyright owner's name)
> in accordance with the provisions of the United States
> Copyright Law."

I (We) acknowledge that I (we) are granted no right to sell, loan or otherwise distribute reproduced copies of the publication other than for the use set down above. No other rights of any kind for any other use are included in this permission.

If you do not grant the above permission, will you supply me (us) with _____ photocopies?_____If so, at what price per copy?_____

_____

By:_____

Accepted and Agreed to:

Address:_____

_____

_____Date: _____

APPENDIX   B2:

REQUEST   FOR   PERMISSION   TO   ARRANGE

STANDARD FORM RECOMMENDED BY:

Music Educators National Conference, Music Teachers National Association, National Association of Jazz Educators, National Association of Schools of Music, Music Publishers' Association of the USA and National Music Publishers' Association.

REQUEST FOR PERMISSION TO ARRANGE
PART I
INSTRUCTIONS

This form is to be prepared in duplicate. After completing Part I and signing both copies where indicated, forward both to the publisher who will complete Part II of the form and return it to you. If the publisher indicates a payment for the right you request, and if the conditions are agreeable to you, remit the amount to the publisher together with the original copy, which he will have signed, whereupon the agreement will be completed.

To:_____Date:_____
(Name of Publisher)

_____
(Address of Publisher)

Gentlemen:

    We hereby request your permission and non-exclusive license to arrange the following musical composition:

_____

    By:_____(words)

        _____(music)

(hereinafter referred to as "The Arrangement")

1. The Arrangement will be for_____in
(type of arrangement)

_____. We will produce
(number of instrumental and/or vocal parts)

_____copies of The Arrangement for use and performance only by our

_____for which no admission fees shall be charged,
(teachers, students, members, congregation, etc.)

or for performance otherwise exempt under the provision of the U.S. Copyright Law.

2. No right to record or to reproduce additional copies is granted to us. We understand that if we wish to record The Arrangement a separate license will be required. We agree not to distribute (except for use of copies as provided in Paragraph 1), sell, loan or lease copies of The Arrangement to anyone.

PART II

3. All copies of The Arrangement shall bear the following copyright notice and the words "Arranged by Permission":

at the bottom of the first page of music of each part of The Arrangement. We will furnish you with a copy of The Arrangement upon completion.

4. We will have The Arrangement made by a person connected with us as our employee for hire, without any payment obligation on your part, and our signature below, together with yours underneath the words "Permission Granted" below shall assign to you all of our right in The Arrangement and the copyright in The Arrangement together with the sole right of registering the copyright as a work made for hire in your name or the name of your designee.

5. Additional provisions (if applicable):

6. In consideration of your permission to arrange, we will pay you $_____ upon the granting by you of the permission requested.

7. This license agreement sets forth our entire understanding and may not be modified or amended except by written agreement signed by both of us.

Very truly yours,

_____
Name of institution

_____
Address

By:_____

Permission Granted:

By:_____
Publisher

Permission denied because:

☐ 1. Arrangement available for sale.

☐ 2. Arrangement in process of publication for sale.

☐ 3. May not be arranged because of contractual commitments.

☐ 4. Other:_____

_____

APPENDIX   B3:

SELECTED   SOURCES   FOR   FORMS

Association for Multi-Image International, Inc. (AMI)
8019 North Himes Avenue, Suite 401
Tampa, FL 33614
813/932-1692

Benison, Shmuel, ed. *The Producer's Masterguide.* 7th ed. New York: New York Production Manual, 1987.

Entertainment Industry Contracts. New York: Matthew Bender, 1987.

Lindey on Entertainment, Publishing and the Arts. 2nd ed. 3 vols. New York: Clark Boardman, 1984.

Passman, Donald S., ed. *The Music and Recording Industry: Practical and Business Aspects.* Los Angeles: Entertainment Law Institute/University of Southern California Law Center, 1984.

Selz, Thomas, and Simensky, Melvin. *Entertainment Law: Legal Concepts and Business Practices.* 3 vols. Colorado Springs, CO: Shepard's/McGraw-Hill, 1984.

Shemel, Sidney, and Krasilovsky, M. William. *More About This Business of Music.* New York: Billboard, 1974.

Sperber, Philip. *Intellectual Property Management: Law-Business-Strategy.* 3 vols. New York: Clark Boardman, 1983.

APPENDIX   C1:

FAIR   USE   GUIDELINES   FOR   PRINT
MATERIALS

types of copying permitted under these guidelines may not be permissible in the future; and conversely that in the future other types of copying not permitted under these guidelines may be permissible under revised guidelines.

Moreover, the following statement of guidelines is not intended to limit the types of copying permitted under the standards of fair use under judicial decision and which are stated in Section 107 of the Copyright Revision Bill. There may be instances in which copying which does not fall within the guidelines stated below may nonetheless be permitted under the criteria of fair use.

(ii) Guidelines With Respect to Books and Periodicals

In a joint letter to Chairman Kastenmeier, dated March 19, 1976, the representatives of the Ad Hoc Committee of Educational Institutions and Organizations on Copyright Law Revision, and of the Authors League of America, Inc., and the Association of American Publishers, Inc., stated:

> You may remember that in our letter of March 8, 1976 we told you that the negotiating teams representing authors and publishers and the Ad Hoc Group had reached tentative agreement on guidelines to insert in the Committee Report covering educational copying from books and periodicals under Section 107 of H.R. 2223 and S. 22, and that as part of that tentative agreement each side would accept the amendments to Sections 107 and 504 which were adopted by your Subcommittee on March 3, 1976.
>
> We are now happy to tell you that the agreement has been approved by the principals and we enclose a copy herewith. We had originally intended to translate the agreement into language suitable for inclusion in the legislative report dealing with Section 107, but we have since been advised by committee staff that this will not be necessary.
>
> As stated above, the agreement refers only to copying from books and periodicals, and it is not intended to apply to musical or audiovisual works.

The full text of the agreement is as follows:

AGREEMENT ON GUIDELINES FOR CLASSROOM COPYING IN
NOT-FOR-PROFIT EDUCATIONAL INSTITUTIONS
WITH RESPECT TO BOOKS AND PERIODICALS

The purpose of the following guidelines is to state the minimum and not the maximum standards of educational fair use under Section 107 of H.R. 2223. The parties agree that the conditions determining the extent of permissible copying for educational purposes may change in the future; that certain

GUIDELINES

I. *Single Copying for Teachers*

A single copy may be made of any of the following by or for a teacher at his or her individual request for his or her scholarly research or use in teaching or preparation to teach a class:

A. A chapter from a book;

B. An article from a periodical or newspaper;

C. A short story, short essay or short poem, whether or not from a collective work;

D. A chart, graph, diagram, drawing, cartoon or picture from a book, periodical, or newspaper;

II. *Multiple Copies for Classroom Use*

Multiple copies (not to exceed in any event more than one copy per pupil in a course) may be made by or for the teacher giving the course for classroom use or discussion; *provided that:*

A. The copying meets the tests of brevity and spontaneity as defined below; *and,*

B. Meets the cumulative effect test as defined below; *and,*

C. Each copy includes a notice of copyright

Definitions

Brevity

(i) Poetry: (a) A complete poem if less than 250 words and if printed on not more than two pages or, (b) from a longer poem, an excerpt of not more than 250 words.

(ii) Prose: (a) Either a complete article, story or essay of less than 2,500 words, or (b) an excerpt from any prose work of not more than 1,000 words or 10% of the work, whichever is less, but in any event a minimum of 500 words.

[Each of the numerical limits stated in "i" and "ii" above may be expanded to permit the completion of an unfinished line of a poem or of an unfinished prose paragraph.]

(iii) Illustration: One chart, graph, diagram,

drawing, cartoon or picture per book or per periodical issue.

(iv) "Special" works: Certain works in poetry, prose or in "poetic prose" which often combine language with illustrations and which are intended sometimes for children and at other times for a more general audience fall short of 2,500 words in their entirety. Paragraph "ii" above notwithstanding such "special works" may not be reproduced in their entirety; however, an excerpt comprising not more than two of the published pages of such special work and containing not more than 10% of the words found in the text thereof, may be reproduced.

Spontaneity

(i) The copying is at the instance and inspiration of the individual teacher, and

(ii) The inspiration and decision to use the work and the moment of its use for maximum teaching effectiveness are so close in time that it would be unreasonable to expect a timely reply to a request for permission.

Cumulative Effect

(i) The copying of the material is for only one course in the school in which the copies are made.

(ii) Not more than one short poem, article, story, essay or two excerpts may be copied from the same author, nor more than three from the same collective work or periodical volume during one class term.

(iii) There shall not be more than nine instances of such multiple copying for one course during one class term.

[The limitations stated in "ii" and "iii" above shall not apply to current news periodicals and newspapers and current news sections of other periodicals.]

III. *Prohibitions as to I and II Above*

Notwithstanding any of the above, the following shall be prohibited:

(A) Copying shall not be used to create or to replace or substitute for anthologies, compilations or collective works. Such replacement or substitution may occur whether copies of various works or excerpts therefrom are accumulated or reproduced and used separately.

(B) There shall be no copying of or from works intended to be "consumable" in the course of study or of teaching. These include workbooks, exercises, standardized tests and test booklets and answer sheets and like consumable material.

(C) Copying shall not:
(a) substitute for the purchase of books, publishers' reprints or periodicals;
(b) be directed by higher authority;

(c) be repeated with respect to the same item by the same teacher from term to term.

(D) No charge shall be made to the student beyond the actual cost of the photocopying.

Agreed MARCH 19, 1976.

Ad Hoc Committee on Copyright Law Revision:
By SHELDON ELLIOTT STEINBACH.

Author-Publisher Group:

Authors League of America:
By IRWIN KARP, *Counsel.*

Association of American Publishers, Inc.:
By ALEXANDER C. HOFFMAN,
Chairman, Copyright Committee.

APPENDIX C2:

FAIR USE GUIDELINES FOR MUSIC

(iii) Guidelines With Respect to Music

In a joint letter dated April 30, 1976, representatives of the Music Publishers' Association of the United States, Inc., the National Music Publishers' Association, Inc., the Music Teachers National Association, the Music Educators National Conference, the National Association of Schools of Music, and the Ad Hoc Committee on Copyright Law Revision, wrote to Chairman Kastenmeier as follows:

During the hearings on H.R. 2223 in June 1975, you and several of your subcommittee members suggested that concerned groups should work together in developing guidelines which would be helpful to clarify Section 107 of the bill.

Representatives of music educators and music publishers delayed their meetings until guidelines had been developed relative to books and periodicals. Shortly after that work was completed and those guidelines were forwarded to your subcommittee, representatives of the undersigned music organizations met together with representatives of the Ad Hoc Committee on Copyright Law Revision to draft guidelines relative to music.

We are very pleased to inform you that the discussions thus have been fruitful on the guidelines which have been developed. Since private music teachers are an important factor in music education, due consideration has been given to the concerns of that group.

We trust that this will be helpful in the report on the bill to clarify Fair Use as it applies to music.

The text of the guidelines accompanying this letter is as follows:

GUIDELINES FOR EDUCATIONAL USES OF MUSIC

The purpose of the following guidelines is to state the minimum and not the maximum standards of educational fair use under Section 107 of HR 2223. The parties agree that the conditions determining the extent of permissible copying for educational purposes may change in the future; that certain types of copying permitted under these guidelines may not be permissible in the future, and conversely that in the future other types of copying not permitted under these guidelines may be permissible under revised guidelines.

Moreover, the following statement of guidelines is not intended to limit the types of copying permitted under the standards of fair use under judicial decision and which are stated in Section 107 of the Copyright Revision Bill. There may be instances in which copying which does not fall within the guidelines stated below may nonetheless be permitted under the criteria of fair use.

A. Permissible Uses

1. Emergency copying to replace purchased copies which for any reason are not available for an imminent performance provided purchased replacement copies shall be substituted in due course.

2. For academic purposes other than performance, single or multiple copies of excerpts of works may be made, provided that the excerpts do not comprise a part of the whole which would constitute a performable unit such as a section*, movement or aria, but in no case more than 10 percent of the whole work. The number of copies shall not exceed one copy per pupil.**

3. Printed copies which have been purchased may be edited or simplified provided that the fundamental character of the work is not distorted or the lyrics, if any, altered or lyrics added if none exist.

4. A single copy of recordings of performances by students may be made for evaluation or rehearsal purposes and may be retained by the educational institution or individual teacher.

5. A single copy of a sound recording (such as a tape, disc or cassette) of copyrighted music may be made from sound recordings owned by an educational institution or an individual teacher for the purpose of constructing aural exercises or examinations and may be retained by the educational institution or individual teacher. (This pertains only to the copyright of the music itself and not to any copyright which may exist in the sound recording.)

*Corrected from *Congressional Record.*

**Editor's Note:* As reprinted in the House Report, subsection A.2 of the Music Guidelines had consisted of two separate paragraphs, one dealing with multiple copies and a second dealing with single copies. In his introductory remarks during the House debates on S.22, the Chairman of the House Judiciary Subcommittee, Mr. Kastenmeier, announced that "the report, as printed, does not reflect a subsequent change in the joint guidelines which was described in a subsequent letter to me from a representative of [the signatory organizations]," and provided the revised text of subsection A.2. (122 *CONG. REC.* H 10875, Sept. 22, 1976). The text reprinted here is the revised text.

B. Prohibitions

1. Copying to create or replace or substitute for anthologies, compilations or collective works.

2. Copying of or from works intended to be "consumable" in the course of study or of teaching such as workbooks, exercises, standardized tests and answer sheets and like material.

3. Copying for the purpose of performance, except as in A (1) above.

4. Copying for the purpose of substituting for the purchase of music, except as in A(1) and A(2) above.

5. Copying without inclusion of the copyright notice which appears on the printed copy.

APPENDIX   C3:

FAIR   USE   GUIDELINES
FOR   OFF-AIR   TAPING

FAIR USE GUIDELINES for OFF-AIR VIDEOTAPING

In March of 1979, Congressman Robert Kastenmeier, chairman of the House Subcommittee on Courts, Civil Liberties, and Administration of Justice, appointed a Negotiating Committee consisting of representatives of education organizations, copyright proprietors, and creative guild and unions. The following guidelines reflect the Negotiating Committee's consensus as to the application of "fair use" to the recording, retention, and use of television broadcast programs for educational purposes. They specify periods of retention and use of such off-air recordings in classrooms and similar places devoted to instruction and for homebound instruction. The purpose of establishing these guidelines is to provide standards for both owners and users of copyrighted television programs.

GUIDELINES FOR OFF-AIR RECORDING OF BROADCAST PROGRAMMING FOR EDUCATIONAL PURPOSES

1. The guidelines were developed to apply only to off-air recording by nonprofit educational institutions.

2. A broadcast program may be recorded off-air simultaneously with broadcast transmission (including simultaneous cable retransmission) and retained by a nonprofit educational institution for a period not to exceed the first forty-five (45) consecutive calendar days after date of recording. Upon conclusion of such retention period, all off-air recordings must be erased or destroyed immediately. "Broadcast programs" are television programs transmitted by television stations for reception by the general public without charge.

3. Off-air recordings may be used once by individual teachers in the course of relevant teaching activities, and repeated once only when instructional reinforcement is necessary, in classrooms and similar places devoted to instruction within a single building, cluster or campus, as well as in the homes of students receiving formalized home instruction, during the first ten (10) consecutive school days in the forty-five (45) day calendar day retention period. "School days" are school session days—not counting weekends, holidays, vacations, examination periods, and other scheduled interruptions—within the forty-five (45) calendar day retention period.

4. Off-air recordings may be made only at the request of and used by individual teachers, and may not be regularly recorded in anticipation of requests. No broadcast program may be recorded off-air more than once at the request of the same teacher, regardless of the number of times the program may be broadcast.

5. A limited number of copies may be reproduced from each off-air recording to meet the legitimate needs of teachers under these guidelines. Each such additional copy shall be subject to all provision governing the original recording.

6. After the first ten (10) consecutive school days, off-air recordings may be used up to the end of the forty-five (45) calendar day retention period only for teacher evaluation purposes i.e., to determine whether or not to include the broadcast program in the teaching curriculum, and may not be used in the recording institution for student exhibition or any other non-evaluation purpose without authorization.

7. Off-air recordings need not be used in their entirety, but the recorded programs may not be altered from their original content. Off-air recordings may not be physically or electronically combined or merged to constitute teaching anthologies or compilations.

8. All copies of off-air recording must include the copyright notice on the broadcast program as recorded.

9. Educational institutions are expected to establish appropriate control procedures to maintain the integrity of these guidelines.

APPENDIX   D1:

R31–IDEAS,   METHODS,   OR   SYSTEMS

R31

Circular

Ideas, Methods, or Systems

WHAT IS NOT PROTECTED BY COPYRIGHT

Ideas, Methods, or Systems are not subject to copyright protection. Copyright protection therefore is not available for: ideas or procedures for doing, making, or building things; scientific or technical methods or discoveries; business operations or procedures; mathematical principles; formulas; algorithms; or any other sort of concept, process, or method of operation.

Section 102 of the copyright law, title 17, United States Code, clearly expresses this principle, "In no case does copyright protection for an original work of authorship extend to any idea, procedure, process, system, method of operation, concept, principle, or discovery, regardless of the form in which it is described, explained, illustrated, or embodied in such work."

Inventions are subject matter for patents, not copyrights. Under certain circumstances it may be possible to secure patent protection for an invention or an inventive design for an article of manufacture. You can obtain general information about the standards and conditions of the patent laws by writing to the Commissioner of Patents and Trademarks, Washington, D.C. 20231.

WHAT IS PROTECTED BY COPYRIGHT

Copyright protection extends to a description, explanation, or illustration of an idea or system, assuming that the requirements of the copyright law are met. Copyright in such a case protects the particular literary or pictorial expression chosen by the author. However, it gives the copyright owner no exclusive rights in the idea, method, or system involved.

Suppose, for example, that an author writes a book explaining a new system for food processing. The copyright in the book, which comes into effect at the moment the work is fixed in a tangible form, will prevent others from publishing the text and illustrations describing the author's ideas for machinery, processes, and merchandising methods. However, it will not give the author any rights against others who adopt the ideas for commercial purposes, or who develop or use the machinery, processes, or methods described in the book.

NO COMPARATIVE SEARCHES

The Copyright Office ordinarily does not compare deposit copies or check registration records to determine whether works submitted for registration are similar to any material for which a registration of a copyright claim has already been made. The records of the Copyright Office may contain any number of registrations for works describing or illustrating the same idea.

162

APPENDIX   D2:

R32—BLANK   FORMS   AND   OTHER   WORKS   NOT   PROTECTED   BY   COPYRIGHT

Blank Forms and Other Works Not Protected by Copyright

Blank forms and similar works, designed to record rather than to convey information, cannot be protected by copyright.

In order to be protected by copyright, a work must contain at least a certain minimum amount of original literary, pictoral, or musical expression. Copyright does not extend to names, titles, and short phrases or clauses such as column headings or simple checklists. The format, arrangement, or typography of a work is not protected. Furthermore, copyright protection does not extend to works consisting entirely of information that is common property containing no original authorship; for example: standard calendars, height and weight charts, tape measures and rulers, schedules of sporting events, and lists or tables taken from public documents or other common sources.

It is only the actual expression of the author that can be protected by copyright. The ideas, plans, methods, or systems described or embodied in a work are not protected by copyright. Thus, there would be no way to secure copyright protection for the idea or principle behind a blank form or similar work, or for any of the methods or systems involved in it.

An original literary or pictorial work is subject to copyright registration even though it is published in conjunction with a blank form or other material not protected by copyright, provided that the requirements of the copyright law have been met. However, copyright in such a case would extend protection only to the original literary or pictorial expression used by the author, as distinguished from the blank form or other unprotected aspects of the work. Example: original photographs published in conjunction with a blank form, or "a compilation of terms or phrases."

APPENDIX   D3:

R34—COPYRIGHT   PROTECTION   NOT AVAILABLE   FOR   NAMES,   TITLES, OR   SHORT   PHRASES

Copyright Primer

R34

Copyright Protection Not Available For Names, Titles, or Short Phrases

---

SHORT EXPRESSIONS NOT PROTECTED BY COPYRIGHT

Names, titles, and short phrases or expressions are not subject to copyright protection. Even if a name, title, or short phrase is novel, distinctive, or lends itself to a play on words, it cannot be protected by copyright. The Copyright Office cannot register claims to exclusive rights in brief combinations of words, such as:

- Names of products or services;
- Names of businesses, organizations, or groups (including the name of a group of performers);
- Names or pseudonyms of individuals (including a pen name or stage name);
- Titles of works;
- Catchwords, catch phrases, mottoes, slogans, or short advertising expressions;
- Mere listings of ingredients, as in a recipe or formula; however, when a recipe or formula is accompanied by substantial literary expression in the form of explanation or directions, or when there is a compilation of recipes, there may be a basis for copyright protection.

SUBJECT MATTER OF COPYRIGHT

Copyright protection under the copyright law (title 17 of the United States Code, section 102) extends only to "ori-

ginal works of authorship." The statute states clearly that ideas and concepts cannot be protected by copyright. To be protected by copyright, a work must contain at least a certain minimum amount of authorship in the form of original literary, musical, or graphic expression. Names, titles, and other short phrases do not meet these requirements.

COPYRIGHT OFFICE RECORDS: WHY TITLES ARE LISTED

The titles of registered works are filed alphabetically and appear in that order in the indexes and catalogs of the Copyright Office.

However, the presence of a title in the Copyright Office registration records does not mean that the title itself is copyrighted or subject to copyright protection. In many cases, our records show the same or closely similar titles for entirely different works.

PROTECTION UNDER TRADEMARK OR UNFAIR COMPETITION LAWS

Some brand names, trade names, slogans, and phrases may be entitled to protection under the general rules of law relating to unfair competition, or to registration under the provisions of the trademark laws. The Copyright Office has no jurisdiction in these matters. Questions about the trademark laws should be addressed to the Commissioner of Patents and Trademarks, Washington, D.C. 20231.

APPENDIX   D4:

R96(SECTION   201.20)—METHODS   OF
AFFIXATION   AND   POSITIONS   OF   THE
COPYRIGHT   NOTICE   ON   VARIOUS
TYPES   OF   WORKS

Copyright Primer

Circular

§201.20, 37 C.F.R.
**Methods of
Affixation and
Positions of the
Copyright Notice
on Various Types
of Works***

Section
201.20

Final Regulation. Part 201 of 37 C.F.R. Chapter II is amended by adding a new §201.20 to read as follows:

§201.20   **Methods of affixation and positions of the copyright notice on various types of works.**

(a) **GENERAL.**

(1) This section specifies examples of methods of affixation and positions of the copyright notice on various types of works that will satisfy the notice requirement of section 401(c) of title 17 of the United States Code, as amended by Pub. L. 94-553. A notice considered "acceptable" under this regulation shall be considered to satisfy the requirement of that section that it be "affixed to the copies in such manner and location as to give reasonable notice of the claim of copyright." As provided by that section, the examples specified in this regulation shall not be considered exhaustive of methods of affixation and positions giving reasonable notice of the claim of copyright.

(2) The provisions of this section are applicable to copies publicly distributed on or after December 1, 1981. This section does not establish any rules concerning the form of the notice or the legal sufficiency of particular notices, except with respect to methods of affixation and positions of notice. The adequacy or legal sufficiency of a copyright notice is determined by the law in effect at the time of first publication of the work.

(b) **DEFINITIONS.**

For the purposes of this section:
(1) The terms "audiovisual works," "collective works," "copies," "device," "fixed," "machine," "motion picture," "pictorial, graphic, and sculptural works," and their variant forms, have the meanings given to them in section 101 of title 17.
(2) "Title 17" means title 17 of the United States Code,

*This final regulation with supplementary information was published in the FEDERAL REGISTER (46 Fed. Reg. 58307) on December 1, 1981. The notice of proposed rulemaking was published in the FEDERAL REGISTER on December 23, 1977. Codified in 37 C.F.R. §201.20 (1982). This regulation was originally published by the Copyright Office as Announcement ML-268.

as amended by Pub. L. 94-553.

(3) In the case of a work consisting preponderantly of leaves on which the work is printed or otherwise reproduced on both sides, a "page" is one side of a leaf; where the preponderance of the leaves are printed on one side only, the terms "page" and "leaf" mean the same.

(4) A work is published in "book form" if the copies embodying it consist of multiple leaves bound, fastened, or assembled in a predetermined order, as, for example, a volume, booklet, pamphlet, or multipage folder. For the purpose of this section, a work need not consist of textual matter in order to be considered published in "book form."

(5) A "title page" is a page, or two consecutive pages facing each other, appearing at or near the front of the copies of a work published in book form, on which the complete title of the work is prominently stated and on which the names of the author or authors, the name of the publisher, the place of publication, or some combination of them, are given.

(6) The meaning of the terms "front," "back," "first," "last," and "following," when used in connection with works published in book form, will vary in relation to the physical form of the copies, depending upon the particular language in which the work is written.

(7) In the case of a work published in book form with a hard or soft cover, the "front page" and "back page" of the copies are the outsides of the front and back covers; where there is no cover, the "front page," and "back page" are the pages visible at the front and back of the copies before they are opened.

(8) A "masthead" is a body of information appearing in approximately the same location in most issues of a newspaper, magazine, journal, review, or other periodical or serial, typically containing the title of the periodical or serial, information about the staff, periodicity of issues, operation, and subscription and editorial policies, of the publication.

(9) A "single-leaf work" is a work published in copies consisting of a single leaf, including copies on which the work is printed or otherwise reproduced on either one side or on both sides of the leaf, and also folders which, without cutting or tearing the copies, can be opened out to form a single leaf. For the purpose of this section, a work need not consist of textual matter in order to be considered a "single-leaf work."

(c) MANNER OF AFFIXATION AND POSITION GENERALLY.

(1) In all cases dealt with in this section, the acceptability of a notice depends upon its being permanently legible to an ordinary user of the work under normal conditions of use, and affixed to the copies in such manner and position that, when affixed, it is not concealed from view upon reasonable examination.

(2) Where, in a particular case, a notice does not appear in one of the precise locations prescribed in this section but a person looking in one of those locations would be reasonably certain to find a notice in another somewhat different location, that notice will be acceptable under this section.

(d) WORKS PUBLISHED IN BOOK FORM.

In the case of works published in book form, a notice reproduced on the copies in any of the following positions is acceptable:

(1) The title page, if any;

(2) The page immediately following the title page, if any;

(3) Either side of the front cover, if any; or, if there is no front cover, either side of the front leaf of the copies;

(4) Either side of the back cover, if any; or, if there is no back cover, either side of the back leaf of the copies;

(5) The first page of the main body of the work;

(6) The last page of the main body of the work;

(7) Any page between the front page and the first page of the main body of the work, if: (i) There are no more than ten pages between the front page and the first page of the main body of the work; and (ii) the notice is reproduced prominently and is set apart from other matter on the page where it appears;

(8) Any page between the last page of the main body of the work and back page, if: (i) There are no more than ten pages between the last page of the main body of the work and the back page; and (ii) the notice is reproduced prominently and is set apart from the other matter on the page where it appears.

(9) In the case of a work published as an issue of a periodical or serial, in addition to any of the locations listed in paragraphs (d)(1) through (8) of this section, a notice is acceptable if it is located: (i) As a part of, or adjacent to, the masthead; (ii) on the page containing the masthead if the

notice is reproduced prominently and is set apart from the other matter appearing on the page; or (iii) adjacent to a prominent heading, appearing at or near the front of the issue, containing the title of the periodical or serial and any combination of the volume and issue number and date of the issue.

(10) In the case of a musical work, in addition to any of the locations listed in paragraphs (d)(1) through (9) of this section, a notice is acceptable if it is located on the first page of music.

(e) SINGLE-LEAF WORKS.

In the case of single-leaf works, a notice reproduced on the copies anywhere on the front or back of the leaf is acceptable.

(f) CONTRIBUTIONS TO COLLECTIVE WORKS.

For a separate contribution to a collective work to be considered to "bear its own notice of copyright," as provided by 17 U.S.C. 404, a notice reproduced on the copies in any of the following positions is acceptable:

(1) Where the separate contribution is reproduced on a single page, a notice is acceptable if it appears: (i) Under the title of the contribution on that page; (ii) adjacent to the contribution; or (iii) on the same page if, through format, wording, or both, the application of the notice to the particular contribution is made clear;

(2) Where the separate contribution is reproduced on more than one page of the collective work, a notice is acceptable if it appears: (i) Under a title appearing at or near the beginning of the contribution; (ii) on the first page of the main body of the contribution; (iii) immediately following the end of the contribution; or (iv) on any of the pages where the contribution appears, if: (A) The contribution is reproduced on no more than twenty pages of the collective work; (B) the notice is reproduced prominently and is set apart from other matter on the page where it appears; and (C) through format, wording, or both, the application of the notice to the particular contribution is made clear;

(3) Where the separate contribution is a musical work, in addition to any of the locations listed in paragraphs (f)(1) and (2) of this section, a notice is acceptable if it is located on the first page of music of the contribution;

(4) As an alternative to placing the notice on one of the pages where a separate contribution itself appears, the contribution is considered to "bear its own notice" if the no-

tice appears clearly in juxtaposition with a separate listing of the contribution by title, or if the contribution is untitled, by a description reasonably identifying the contribution: (i) On the page bearing the copyright notice for the collective work as a whole, if any; or (ii) in a clearly identified and readily-accessible table of contents or listing of acknowledgements appearing near the front or back of the collective work as a whole.

(g) WORKS REPRODUCED IN MACHINE-READABLE COPIES.

For works reproduced in machine-readable copies (such as magnetic tapes or disks, punched cards, or the like, from which the work cannot ordinarily be visually perceived except with the aid of a machine or device,[1] each of the following constitute examples of acceptable methods of affixation and position of notice:

(1) A notice embodied in the copies in machine-readable form in such a manner that on visually perceptible printouts it appears either with or near the title, or at the end of the work;

(2) A notice that is displayed at the user's terminal at sign on;

(3) A notice that is continuously on terminal display; or

(4) A legible notice reproduced durably, so as to withstand normal use, on a gummed or other label securely affixed to the copies or to a box, reel, cartridge, cassette, or other container used as a permanent receptacle for the copies.

(h) MOTION PICTURES AND OTHER AUDIOVISUAL WORKS.

(1) The following constitute examples of acceptable methods of affixation and positions of the copyright notice on motion pictures and other audiovisual works: A notice that is embodied in the copies by a photomechanical or electronic process, in such a position that it ordinarily would appear whenever the work is performed in its entirety, and

---

[1] Works published in a form requiring the use of a machine or device for purposes of optical enlargement (such as film, filmstrips, slide films, and works published in any variety of microform) and works published in visually perceptible form but used in connection with optical scanning devices, are not within this category.

that is located: (i) With or near the title; (ii) with the cast, credits, and similar information; (iii) at or immediately following the beginning of the work; or (iv) at or immediately preceding the end of the work.

(2) In the case of an untitled motion picture or other audiovisual work whose duration is sixty seconds or less, in addition to any of the locations listed in paragraph (h)(1) of this section, a notice that is embodied in the copies by a photomechanical or electronic process, in such a position that it ordinarily would appear to the projectionist or broadcaster when preparing the work for performance, is acceptable if it is located on the leader of the film or tape immediately preceding the beginning of the work.

(3) In the case of a motion picture or other audiovisual work that is distributed to the public for private use, the notice may be affixed, in addition to the locations specified in paragraph (h)(1) of this section, on the housing or container, if it is a permanent receptacle for the work.

(i) PICTORIAL, GRAPHIC, AND SCULPTURAL WORKS.

The following constitute examples of acceptable methods of affixation and positions of the copyright notice on various forms of pictorial, graphic, and sculptural works:

(1) Where a work is reproduced in two-dimensional copies, a notice affixed directly or by means of a label cemented, sewn, or otherwise attached durably, so as to withstand normal use, of the front or back of the copies, or to any backing, mounting, matting, framing, or other material to which the copies are durably attached, so as to withstand normal use, or in which they are permanently housed, is acceptable.

(2) Where a work is reproduced in three-dimensional copies, a notice affixed directly or by means of a label cemented, sewn, or otherwise attached durably, so as to withstand normal use, to any visible portion of the work, or to any base, mounting, framing, or other material on which the copies are durably attached, so as to withstand normal use, or in which they are permanently housed, is acceptable.

(3) Where, because of the size or physical characteristics of the material in which the work is reproduced in copies, it is impossible or extremely impracticable to affix a notice to the copies directly or by means of a durable label, a notice is acceptable if it appears on a tag that is of durable material, so as to withstand normal use, and that is attached to the copy with sufficient durability that it will remain with the copy while it is passing through its normal

channels of commerce.

(4) Where a work is reproduced in copies consisting of sheet-like or strip material bearing multiple or continuous reproductions of the work, the notice may be applied: (i) To the reproduction itself; (ii) to the margin, selvage, or reverse side of the material at frequent and regular intervals; or (iii) if the material contains neither a selvage nor a reverse side, to tags or labels, attached to the copies and to any spools, reels, or containers housing them in such a way that a notice is visible while the copies are passing through their normal channels of commerce.

(5) If the work is permanently housed in a container, such as a game or puzzle box, a notice reproduced on the permanent container is acceptable.

(17 U.S.C. 401, 702)

[46 FR 58312, Dec. 1, 1981]

APPENDIX   D5:

R40b(excerpt)—DEPOSIT REQUIREMENTS FOR   VISUAL   ARTS   MATERIALS

TWO-DIMENSIONAL WORKS

Nature of Work	Required Deposit	
	Published	**Unpublished**
Advertisements	Page containing published advertisement (proofs *not* acceptable)	Photocopy, proof, drawing, copy, or layout
Blueprints, architectural drawings, mechanical drawings, diagrams	1 complete copy	1 copy
Book jackets or record jackets	1 complete copy	1 copy
Commercial print or label (for example, flyers, labels, or catalogs used in connection with the sale of goods or services)	1 complete copy	1 copy
Fabric, textile, wallpaper, carpeting, floor tile, wrapping paper, yard goods	1 complete copy (or swatch) showing the design repeat and copyright notice	1 complete copy (or I.D. material if the work has not been fixed in repeat)
Fabric emblems or patches, decals or heat transfers (not applied to clothing), bumper stickers	2 complete copies	1 copy or I.D. material
Greeting cards, picture postcards, stationery, business cards	1 complete copy	1 copy or I.D. material
Maps or cartographic material	2 complete copies	1 copy or I.D. material
Patterns, cross-stitch graphs, stitchery brochures	2 complete copies	1 copy or I.D. material
Photographs, drawings, cartoons, etc., published as part of a collective work such as a periodical or anthology	1 complete copy of the collective work or one copy of the newspaper section in which published	
Pictorial or graphic works (for example, artwork, drawings, illustrations, paintings)	2 complete copies	1 copy or I.D. material
Posters, photographs, prints, brochures, exhibition catalogs, calendars	2 complete copies	Copy or proofs, photocopy, contact sheets
"Limited edition" poster or prints (published in quantities of fewer than 5 copies, or 300 or fewer numbered copies)	1 copy or I.D. material if individual author is claimant; otherwise, 2 copies	
Oversize material (exceeding 96″ in any dimension)	I.D. material	I.D. material

THREE-DIMENSIONAL WORKS

Nature of Work	Required Deposit	
	Published	**Unpublished**
Artwork or illustrations on 3-D objects (for example, artwork on plates, mugs)	I.D. material	I.D. material
Artwork for a T-shirt (for example, heat transfers or decals already applied to T-shirts)	I.D. material (T-shirt not acceptable)	I.D. material
Fabric or textile attached to or part of a 3-D object	I.D. material	I.D. material
Games—containing 3 or more separately copyrightable 3-dimensional elements in a box not larger than 12" x 24" x 6"	1 complete copy	I.D. material
Games with fewer than 3 separately copyrightable 3-dimensional elements or larger than 12" x 24" x 6"	I.D. material	I.D. material
Globes, relief models, or relief maps	1 complete copy including the stand (I.D. material *not* acceptable)	1 complete copy or I.D. material
Pictorial matter and/or text on a box or container (contents of container are not claimed)	1 copy of box or container if it can be flattened or 1 paper label	1 copy or I.D. material
Prints or labels inseparable from a 3-dimensional object (for example, silk screen label on a bottle, silk screen on a T-shirt)	I.D. material	I.D. material
Sculptures, toys, jewelry, dolls, molds, relief plaques, statues, campaign buttons	I.D. material	I.D. material
Sculpture (for example, doll) in a box with copyrightable pictorial and/or textual material; claim in sculpture and artwork/text	I.D. material for sculpture plus 1 copy of box and any other printed material	I.D. material for sculpture plus copy of box or I.D. material
Stitchery kits, needlework kits	2 complete copies as published	1 copy or I.D. material
Oversize material (exceeding 96" in any dimension)	I.D. material	I.D. material

APPENDIX   D6:

R2 (excerpt)—COPYRIGHT   APPLICATION   FORMS

APPLICATION FORMS

For Original Registration

Form TX: for published and unpublished nondramatic literary works

Form SE: for serials, works issued or intended to be issued in successive parts bearing numerical or chronological designations and intended to be continued indefinitely (periodicals, newspapers, magazines, newsletters, annuals, journals, etc.)

Form PA: for published and unpublished works of the performing arts (musical and dramatic works, pantomimes and choreographic works, motion pictures and other audiovisual works)

Form VA: for published and unpublished works of the visual arts (pictorial, graphic, and sculptural works)

Form SR: for published and unpublished sound recordings

For Renewal Registration

Form RE: for claims to renewal copyright in works copyrighted under the law in effect through December 31, 1977 (1909 Copyright Act)

For Corrections and Amplifications

Form CA: for supplementary registration to correct or amplify information given in the Copyright Office record of an earlier registration

For Continuations

Form VA/CON: for continuation of Form VA, spaces 1, 2, 4, 6

Form TX/CON: for continuation of Form TX and Form SE, spaces 1, 2, 4, 6, 7

Form PA/CON: for continuation of Form PA, spaces 1, 2, 4, 6

Form SR/CON: for continuation of Form SR, spaces 1, 2, 4, 6

Form RE/CON: for continuation of Form RE, space 5

FORMS AND CIRCULARS HOTLINE

NOTE: Requestors may order application forms or circulars at any time by telephoning (202) 287-9100. Orders will be recorded automatically and filled as quickly as possible.

179

APPENDIX D7:

R56(excerpt)—FORM PA VS. FORM SR

How the work was created; what is being registered:	Form to use:	How to describe the authorship in space 2, "Nature of Authorship":	What should be deposited:	
			Published	**Unpublished**
Composer/author creates a song, wishes to claim copyright in the song	PA	Music and Words	2 complete copies (sheet music, etc.) or phonorecords, (usually disks, tapes, cassettes, etc.) of "best edition"	1 complete copy (lead sheet, etc.) or phonorecord, (usually disk, tape, cassette, etc.)
Composer/author creates musical composition, wishes to claim copyright in the musical composition	PA	Music	2 complete copies (sheet music, etc.) or phonorecords, (usually disks, tapes, cassettes, etc.) of "best edition"	1 complete copy (lead sheet, etc.) or phonorecord, (usually disk, tape, cassette, etc.)
Performer(s) (for example, vocalist and band) perform and record musical work; wish to claim copyright in the recorded performance only	SR	Performance and Sound Recording	2 complete phonorecords of "best edition"	1 complete phonorecord
Composer/author/performer creates music and performs it, recording the performance; wishes to claim copyright both in the music and the recording	SR	Music and Performance OR Music, Words, Performance	2 complete phonorecords of "best edition"	1 complete phonorecord
Author writes poem and records it, wishes to claim copyright only in the poem itself, not in recorded performance	TX	Text	2 complete copies or phonorecords of "best edition"	1 complete copy or phonorecord
Author writes a play and records it, wishes to claim copyright only in the play itself, not in recorded performance	PA	Script	2 complete copies or phonorecords of "best edition"	1 complete copy or phonorecord
Author writes poem or narrative and records it, wishes to claim copyright both in the text and in the recorded performance	SR	Text and Sound Recording	2 complete phonorecords of "best edition"	1 complete phonorecord

APPENDIX   D8:

R22(excerpt)—HOW   TO   INVESTIGATE
THE   COPYRIGHT   STATUS   OF   A   WORK

How to Investigate the Copyright Status of a Work

IN GENERAL

Methods of Approaching a Copyright Investigation

There are several ways to investigate whether a work is under copyright protection and, if so, the facts of the copyright. These are the main ones:

1. Examine a copy of the work (or, if the work is a sound recording, examine the disk, tape cartridge, or cassette in which the recorded sound is fixed, or the album cover, sleeve, or container in which the recording is sold) for such elements as a copyright notice, place and date of publication, author and publisher (for additional information, see p. 6, "Copyright Notice");

2. Make a search of the Copyright Office catalogs and other records; or

3. Have the Copyright Office make a search for you.

A Few Words of Caution About Copyright Investigations

Copyright investigations often involve more than one of these methods. Even if you follow all three approaches, the results may not be completely conclusive. Moreover, as explained in this circular, the changes brought about under the Copyright Act of 1976 must be considered when investigating the copyright status of a work.

This circular offers some practical guidance on what to look for if you are making a copyright investigation. It is important to realize, however, that this circular contains only general information, and that there are a number of exceptions to the principles outlined here. In many cases it is important to consult a copyright attorney before reaching any conclusions regarding the copyright status of a work.

HOW TO GO ABOUT SEARCHING COPYRIGHT OFFICE CATALOGS AND RECORDS

Catalog of Copyright Entries

The Copyright Office publishes the *Catalog of Copyright Entries (CCE)*, which is divided into parts according to the classes of works registered. The present categories include: "Nondramatic Literary Works," "Performing Arts," "Motion Pictures and Filmstrips," "Sound Recordings," "Serials and Periodicals," "Visual Arts," "Maps," and "Renewals." Effective with the Fourth Series, Volume 2, 1979 Catalogs, the CCE has been issued in microfiche form **only;** previously, each part of the *Catalog* was issued at regular intervals in book form. Each CCE segment covers all registrations made during a particular period of time. Renewals made for any class during a particular period can be found in Part 8, "Renewals."

Before 1978, the catalog parts reflected the classes that existed at that time. Renewals for a particular class are found in the back section of the catalog for the class of work renewed (for example, renewal registrations for music made in 1976 appear in the last section of the music catalog for 1976).

A number of libraries throughout the United States maintain copies of the *Catalog*, and this may provide a good starting point if you wish to make a search yourself. There are some cases, however, in which a search of the *Catalog* alone will not be sufficient to provide the needed information. For example:

- Since the *Catalog* does not include entries for assignments or other recorded documents, it cannot be used for searches involving the ownership of rights.

- There is usually a time lag of a year or more before the part of the *Catalog* covering a particular registration is published.

- The *Catalog* entry contains the essential facts concerning a registration, but it is not a verbatim transcript of the registration record.

3

Individual Searches of Copyright Records

The Copyright Office is located in the Library of Congress James Madison Memorial Building, 101 Independence Ave., S.E., Washington, D.C.

Most records of the Copyright Office are open to public inspection and searching from 8:30 a.m. to 5 p.m. Monday through Friday (except legal holidays). The various records freely available to the public include an extensive card catalog, an automated catalog containing records from 1978 forward, record books, and microfilm records of assignments and related documents. Other records, including correspondence files and deposit copies, are not open to the public for searching. However, they may be inspected upon request and payment of a $10-per hour search fee.

If you wish to do your own searching in the Copyright Office files open to the public, you will be given assistance in locating the records you need and in learning searching procedures. If the Copyright Office staff actually makes the search for you, a search fee must be charged.

SEARCHING BY THE COPYRIGHT OFFICE

In General

Upon request, the Copyright Office staff will search its records at the statutory rate of $10 for each hour or fraction of an hour consumed. Based on the information you furnish, we will provide an estimate of the total search fee. If you decide to have the Office staff conduct the search, you should send the estimated amount with your request. The Office will then proceed with the search and send you a typewritten report or, if you prefer, an oral report by telephone. If you request an oral report, please provide a telephone number where you can be reached during normal business hours (8:30-5:00).

Search reports can be certified on request, for an extra fee of $4. Certified searches are most frequently requested to meet the evidentiary requirements of litigation.

Your request, and any other correspondence, should be addressed to:

Reference and Bibliography Section, LM-451
Copyright Office
Library of Congress
Washington, D.C. 20559
(202) 287-6850

What the Fee Does Not Cover

Note that the search fee does *not* include the cost of additional certificates, photocopies of deposits, or copies of other office records. For information concerning these services, request Circular R6 from the Copyright Office.

Information Needed

The more detailed information you can furnish with your request, the less time-consuming and expensive the search will be. Please provide as much of the following information as possible:

- The title of the work, with any possible variants;

- The names of the authors, including possible pseudonyms;

- The name of the probable copyright owner, which may be the publisher or producer;

- The approximate year when the work was published or registered;

- The type of work involved (book, play, musical composition, sound recording, photograph, etc.);

- For a work originally published as a part of a periodical or collection, the title of that publication and any other information, such as the volume or issue number, to help identify it;

- Motion pictures are often based on other works such as books or serialized contributions to periodicals or other composite works. If you desire a search for an underlying work or for music from a motion picture, you must specifically request such a search. You must also identify the underlying works and music and furnish the specific titles, authors, and approximate dates of these works; and

- The registration number of any other copyright data.

Searches Involving Assignments and Other Documents Affecting Copyright Ownership

The Copyright Office staff will also, for the standard hourly search fee, search its indexes covering the records of assignments and other recorded documents concerning ownership of copyrights. The reports of searches in these cases will state the facts shown in the Office's indexes of the recorded documents, but will offer no interpretation of the content of the documents or their legal effect.

NOTE: Unless your request specifies otherwise, Copyright Office searches include records pertaining to registrations, renewals, assignments and other recorded documents concerning copyright ownership. If you want the office to search any other special records such as notices of use, or if you want to exclude specific records from your search, please make this clear in your request.

LIMITATIONS ON SEARCHES

In determining whether or not to have a search made, you should keep the following points in mind:

No Special Lists

The Copyright Office does not maintain any listings of works by subject, or any lists of works that are in the public domain.

Contributions

Individual works, such as stories, poems, articles, or musical compositions that were published as contributions to a copyrighted periodical or collection, are usually not listed separately by title in our records.

No Comparisons

The Copyright Office does not search or compare copies of works to determine questions of possible infringement or to determine how much two or more versions of a work have in common.

Titles and Names Not Copyrightable

Copyright does not protect names and titles, and our records list many different works identified by the same or similar titles. Some brand names, trade names, slogans, and phrases may be entitled to protection under the general rules of law relating to unfair competition, or to registration under the provisions of the trademark laws. Questions about the trademark laws should be addressed to the Commissioner of Patents and Trademarks, Washington, D.C. 20231. Possible protection of names and titles under common law principles of unfair competition is a question of state law.

No Legal Advice

The Copyright Office cannot express any opinion as to the legal significance or effect of the facts included in a search report.

SOME WORDS OF CAUTION

Searches Not Always Conclusive

Searches of the Copyright Office catalogs and records are useful in helping to determine the copyright status of a work, but they cannot be regarded as conclusive in all cases. The complete absence of any information about a work in the office records does not mean that the work is unprotected. The following are examples of cases in which information about a particular work may be incomplete or lacking entirely in the Copyright Office:

- Before 1978, unpublished works were entitled to protection at common law without the need of registration.

- Works published with notice prior to 1978 may be registered at **any** time within the first 28-year term; to obtain renewal protection, however, the claimant must register and renew such work by the end of the 28th year.

- For works that came under copyright protection after 1978, registration may be made at any time during the term of protection; it is not generally required as a condition of copyright protection (there are, however, certain definite advantages to registration; please call or write for Circular R1, "Copyright Basics").

- Since searches are ordinarily limited to registrations that have already been cataloged, a search report may not cover recent registrations for which catalog records are not yet available.

- The information in the search request may not have been complete or specific enough to identify the work.

- The work may have been registered under a different title or as part of a larger work.

Protection in Foreign Countries

Even if you conclude that a work is in the public domain in the United States, this does not necessarily mean that you are free to use it in other countries. Every nation has its own

APPENDIX   D9:

R1b—LIMITATIONS   ON   THE
INFORMATION   FURNISHED   BY   THE
COPYRIGHT   OFFICE

Limitations on the Information Furnished by the Copyright Office

The Copyright Office is primarily an office of record: a place where claims to copyright are registered when the claimant has complied with the requirements of the copyright law. We are glad to furnish information about the provisions of the copyright law and the procedures for making registration, to explain the operations and practices of the Copyright Office, and to report on facts found in the public records of the Office. However, the Regulations of the Copyright Office (Code of Federal Regulations, Title 37, Chapter II) prohibit employees from offering legal advice or opinions.

The Copyright Office cannot do any of the following:

—Comment upon the merits, copyright status, or ownership of particular works, or upon the extent of protection afforded to particular works by the copyright law;

—Compare for similarities copies of works deposited for registration or give opinions on the validity of claims;

—Advise on questions of possible copyright infringement or prosecution of copyright violations;

—Draft or interpret contract terms;

—Enforce contracts or recover manuscripts;

—Recommend particular publishers, agents, lawyers, "song services," and the like;

—Help in getting a work published, recorded, or performed.

Many requests for assistance require professional legal advice, frequently that of a copyright expert. However, even though the Copyright Office cannot furnish services of this kind, its policy is to be helpful in supplying the information and services it is authorized to provide.

APPENDIX   D10:

R44—CARTOONS   AND   COMIC   STRIPS

R44

Circular

Cartoons and Comic Strips

IN GENERAL

The copyright law of the United States (title 17 of the United States Code) provides for copyright protection in literary and artistic works. Cartoons and comic strips generally are among the types of works of authorship protected by copyright. This protection extends to any copyrightable pictorial or written expression contained in the work. The title of a cartoon or comic strip is not subject to copyright protection; neither is the general theme for a cartoon or comic strip, nor the general idea or name for the characters depicted. Titles and names may sometimes be protected under state law doctrines or trademark laws, but this type of protection has nothing to do with the copyright statute.

COPYRIGHT REGISTRATION

Cartoons and comic strips may be registered in either published or unpublished form. Registration in the Copyright Office must be made during the first 28-year term of copyright to maintain protection for works published prior to 1978 with a proper copyright notice. While registration is not generally a condition of protection for works first published on or after January 1, 1978, or for unpublished works, there are certain advantages.

The correct application form and deposit for registering a copyright claim depends on the nature of the work and the way in which it is presented. Because a cartoon is generally a work of the visual arts, Form VA is usually appropriate for registration. However, if the textual elements in a comic strip are preponderant, registration should be made on Form TX. If you choose to register your cartoons or comic strips, send the following three elements to the Copyright Office in the same envelope or package:

1. A properly completed application form;

2. A fee of $10 with each application; and

3. A non-returnable deposit of the work to be registered.

DEPOSIT REQUIREMENTS

The deposit requirement for cartoons and comic strips will vary in particular situations. The general requirements are as follows:

- If the work is unpublished, one complete copy.

- If the work was first published in the United States on or after January 1, 1978, two complete copies of the best edition.

- If the work is a contribution to a collective work, and published on or after January 1, 1978, one complete copy of the best edition of the collective work or, in the case of a newspaper, the entire section including the contribution. If published before January 1, 1978, one complete copy of the issue as first published containing the contribution.

- If the work was first published in the United States before January 1, 1978, two complete copies of the work as first published.

- If the work was first published outside the United States whenever published, one complete copy of the work as first published.

Note: If you require further information regarding what to deposit for registration, please write to the Copyright Office.

REGISTRATION OF COLLECTIONS AND CONTRIBUTIONS

A single registration may be made for cartoons published as a unit (for example, a comic book), provided that the copyright claimant is the same for all elements in the unit. Two or more unpublished cartoons or comic strips may be considered for registration as a unit on a single application when submitted with a fee of $10 and a non-returnable deposit of the work if the following conditions are met:

1. The selections are assembled in an orderly form;

2. The combined selections bear a single title identifying the collection as a whole;

3. The copyright claimant in all of the sections, and in the collection as a whole, is the same; and

4. All of the selections are by the same author, or, if they are by different authors, at least one of the authors has contributed copyrightable authorship to each of the selections.

Works registered as a collection will be recorded in the records of the Copyright Office only under the collective title. Copyright registration of cartoons and comic strips extends only to the copyrightable selections deposited at the time of registration. There is no blanket registration that will cover works to be produced in the future.

Copyright Primer

A cartoon or comic strip published as a contribution to a collective work (for example, a periodical or newspaper) may be considered for group registration if certain conditions are met. Please write to the Copyright Office for information and instructions on group registration for contributions to periodicals.

NOTICE OF COPYRIGHT

When a work is published under the authority of the copyright owner, a notice of copyright should be placed on all publicly distributed copies. This notice is required even on works published outside the United States. Failure to comply with the notice requirement can result in the loss of certain additional rights otherwise available to the copyright owner.

The use of the copyright notice is the responsibility of the copyright owner and does not require advance permission from, or registration with, the Copyright Office.

FORM OF NOTICE FOR VISUALLY PERCEPTIBLE COPIES

The notice for visually perceptible copies should contain the following three elements:

1. The symbol © (the letter C in a circle), the word "Copyright," or the abbreviation "Copr.";

2. The year of first publication of the work. In the case of compilations or derivative works incorporating previously published material, the year date of first publication of the compilation or derivative work is sufficient. The year date may be omitted where a pictorial, graphic, or sculptural work, with accompanying textual matter, if any, is reproduced in or on greeting cards, postcards, stationery, jewelry, dolls, toys, or any useful article; and

3. The name of the owner of copyright in the work, or an abbreviation by which the name can be recognized, or a generally known alternative designation of the owner.

190

EXAMPLE: © John Doe 1981

Before 1978, the copyright law required, as a condition for copyright protection, that all copies published with the authorization of the copyright owner bear a proper notice. If a work was published under the copyright owner's authority before January 1, 1978, without a proper copyright notice, all copyright protection for that work was permanently lost in the United States. The new copyright law does not provide retroactive protection for those works.

REGISTRATION PROCESS

The length of time required by the Copyright Office to process an application for registration of a claim to copyright varies from time to time, depending on the amount of such material received and the personnel available to handle it. It must also be kept in mind that it may take a number of days for material to reach the Copyright Office and for the certificate of registration to go by mail from the Copyright Office to the recipient. If examination reveals any problem delaying registration, you will receive correspondence from the examiner responsible for your case.

Please note that registration is effective on the date of receipt in the Copyright Office of all the required elements in acceptable form, regardless of the length of time it takes thereafter to process the material and mail the certificate. If you want to know when the Copyright Office receives your material, you should send it registered or certified mail and request a return receipt.

FURTHER INFORMATION

Any requests for Copyright Office publications and forms or special questions relating to copyright problems not mentioned in this circular should be addressed to the **Information & Publications Section, Copyright Office, Library of Congress, Washington, D.C. 20559.**

APPENDIX   D11:

R22 (excerpt)—COPYRIGHT   NOTICE

laws governing the length and scope of copyright protection, and these are applicable to uses of the work within that nation's borders. Thus, the expiration or loss of copyright protection in the United States may still leave the work fully protected against unauthorized use in other countries.

OTHER CIRCULARS

For further information, request R15, "Renewal of Copyright," R15a, "Duration of Copyright," R15t, "Extension of Copyright Terms," and R6, "Obtaining Copies of Copyright Office Records and Deposits," from:

Publications Section, LM-455
Copyright Office
Library of Congress
Washington, D.C. 20559
OR

You may call 202-287-9100 at any time, day or night, to leave a request for forms or circulars as a recorded message on the Forms HOTLINE. Requests made on the HOTLINE number are filled and mailed promptly.

IMPACT OF COPYRIGHT ACT ON COPYRIGHT INVESTIGATIONS

On October 19, 1976, the President signed into law a complete revision of the copyright law of the United States (Title 17 of the United States Code). Most provisions of the new copyright statute came into force on **January 1, 1978**, superseding the previous copyright act of 1909, and made significant changes in the copyright law. If you need more information about the provisions of the 1976 Act, or if you want a copy of the revised statute, write or call the Copyright Office and request Public Law 94-553.

For copyright investigations, the following are some of the main points to consider about the impact of the Copyright Act of 1976:

A Changed System of Copyright Formalities

Some of the most sweeping changes under the 1976 Act involve copyright formalities; that is, the procedural requirements for securing and maintaining full copyright protection.

The old system of formalities involved copyright notice, deposit and registration, recordation of transfers and licenses of copyright ownership, and United States manufacture, among other things. In general, while retaining formalities the present law reduces the chances of mistakes, softens the consequences of errors and omissions, and allows for the correction of errors.

Automatic Copyright

Under the present copyright law, copyright exists in original works of authorship created and fixed in any tangible medium of expression, now known or later developed, from which they can be perceived, reproduced, or otherwise communicated, either directly, or indirectly with the aid of a machine or device. In other words, copyright is an incident of creative authorship not dependent on statutory formalities. Thus, registration with the Copyright Office generally is not required, but there are certain advantages that arise from a timely registration. For further information on the advantages of registration, write or call the Copyright Office and request Circular R1, "Copyright Basics."

Copyright Notice

Both the 1909 and 1976 copyright acts require a notice of copyright on published works. For most works, a copyright notice consists of the symbol ©, the word "Copyright," or the abbreviation "Copr.," together with the name of the owner of copyright and the year of first publication; for example: "© Marion Crane 1981" or "Copyright 1981 by Milton Arbogast." For sound recordings published on or after February 15, 1972, a copyright notice might read "℗ 1981 XYZ Records, Inc." (See page 8 for more about sound recordings.) The present law prescribes that all visually perceptible published copies of a work, or published phonorecords of a sound recording, shall bear a proper copyright notice. This requirement applies equally whether the work is published in the United States or elsewhere by authority of the copyright owner. Compliance with the statutory notice requirements is the responsibility of the copyright owner. Unauthorized publication without the copyright notice, or with a defective notice, does not affect the validity of the copyright in the work. Advance permission from, or registration with, the Copyright Office is not required before placing a copyright notice on copies of a work, or on phonorecords of a sound recording. Moreover, for works first published on or after January 1, 1978, omission of the required notice, or

6

use of a defective notice, does not result in forfeiture or outright loss of copyright protection. Certain omissions of, or defects in the notice of copyright, however, may lead to loss of copyright protection if certain steps are not taken to correct or cure the omissions or defects. For further information, write to the Copyright Office and request Circular R96 Section 201.20, which contains the regulations on "Methods of Affixation and Positions of the Copyright Notice on Various Types of Works;" the same regulations may also be found in 37 CFR Part 201.

Works Already in the Public Domain

The 1976 Act does not restore protection to works that fell into the public domain before January 1, 1978. If copyright in a particular work has been lost, the work is permanently in the public domain in this country, and the 1976 Act will not revive protection. Under the copyright law in effect prior to January 1, 1978, copyright could be lost in several situations: the most common were publication without the required copyright notice, expiration of the first 28-year copyright term without renewal, or final expiration of the second copyright term.

Scope of Exclusive Rights Under Copyright

The present law has changed and enlarged in some cases, the scope of the copyright owner's rights as against users of a work. The new rights apply to all uses of a work subject to protection by copyright after January 1, 1978, regardless of when the work was created.

DURATION OF COPYRIGHT PROTECTION

Works Originally Copyrighted On or After January 1, 1978

A work that is created and fixed in tangible form for the first time on or after January 1, 1978, is automatically protected from the moment of its creation, and is ordinarily given a term enduring for the author's life, plus an additional 50 years after the author's death. In the case of "a joint work prepared by two or more authors who did not work for hire," the term lasts for 50 years after the last surviving author's death. For works made for hire, and for anonymous and pseudonymous works (unless the author's identity is revealed in Copyright Office records), the duration of copy-

right will be 75 years from publication or 100 years from creation, whichever is less.

Works created before the 1976 law came into effect, but neither published nor registered for copyright before January 1, 1978, have been automatically brought under the statute and are now given Federal copyright protection. The duration of copyright in these works will generally be computed in the same way as for new works: the life-plus-50 or 75/100-year terms will apply. However, all works in this category are guaranteed at least 25 years of statutory protection.

Works Copyrighted Before January 1, 1978

Under the law in effect before 1978, copyright was secured either on the date a work was published with notice of copyright, or on the date of registration if the work was registered in unpublished form. In either case, copyright endured for a first term of 28 years from the date on which it was secured. During the last (28th) year of the first term, the copyright was eligible for renewal. The new copyright law has extended the renewal term from 28 to 47 years for copyrights in existence on January 1, 1978. However, the copyright still must be renewed in the 28th calendar year to receive the 47-year period of added protection. For more detailed information on the copyright term, write or call the Copyright Office and request Circulars R15a and R15t.

WORKS FIRST PUBLISHED BEFORE 1978: THE COPYRIGHT NOTICE

General Information About the Copyright Notice

In investigating the copyright status of works first published before January 1, 1978, the most important thing to look for is the notice of copyright. As a general rule under the previous law, copyright protection was lost permanently if the notice was omitted from the first authorized published edition of a work, or if it appeared in the wrong form or position. The form and position of the copyright notice for various types of works were specified in the copyright statute. Some courts were liberal in overlooking relatively minor departures from the statutory requirements, but a basic failure to comply with the notice provisions forfeited copyright protection and put the work into the public domain in this country.

Absence of Copyright Notice

For works first published before 1978, the complete absence of a copyright notice from a published copy generally indicates that the work is not protected by copyright. However, there are a number of exceptions and qualifications to this general rule. The following are some of them:

Unpublished Works. No notice of copyright was required on the copies of any unpublished work. The concept of "publication" is very technical, and it was possible for a number of copies lacking a copyright notice to be reproduced and distributed without affecting copyright protection.

Foreign Editions. Under certain circumstances, the law exempted copies of a copyrighted work from the notice requirements if they were first published outside the United States. Some copies of these foreign editions could find their way into the United States without impairing the copyright.

Accidental Omission. The 1909 statute preserved copyright protection if the notice was omitted by accident or mistake from a "particular copy or copies."

Unauthorized Publication. A valid copyright was not affected if someone deleted the notice and/or published the work without authorization from the copyright owner.

Sound Recordings. Reproductions of sound recordings usually contain two different types of creative works: the underlying musical, dramatic, or literary work that is being performed or read, and the fixation of the actual sounds embodying the performance or reading. For protection of the underlying musical or literary work embodied in a recording, it is not necessary that a copyright notice covering this material appear on the phonograph records or tapes in which the recording is reproduced. As noted above, a special notice is required for protection of the recording of a series of musical, spoken, or other sounds which were fixed on or after February 15, 1972. Sound recordings fixed before February 15, 1972, are not eligible for Federal copyright protection. Neither the Sound Recording Act of 1971 nor the present copyright law can be applied or be construed to provide any retroactive protection for sound recordings fixed before that date. Such works, however, may be protected by various state laws or doctrines of common law.

The Date in the Copyright Notice

If you find a copyright notice, the date it contains may be important in determining the copyright status of the work. In general, the notice on works published before 1978 must include the year in which copyright was secured by publication (or, if the work was first registered for copyright in unpublished form, the year in which registration was made). There are two main exceptions to this rule.

• For pictorial, graphic, or sculptural works (Classes F through K under the 1909 law) the law permitted omission of the year date in the notice.

• For "new versions" of previously published or copyrighted works, the notice was not usually required to include more than the year of first publication of the new version itself. This is explained further under "Derivative Works" below.

The year in the notice usually (though not always) indicated when the copyright began. It is therefore significant in determining whether a copyright is still in effect; or, if the copyright has not yet run its course, the year date will help in deciding when the copyright is scheduled to expire. For further information about the duration of copyright, request Circular R15a.

In evaluating the meaning of the date in a notice, you should keep the following points in mind:

WORKS PUBLISHED AND COPYRIGHTED BEFORE JANUARY 1, 1978: A work published before January 1, 1978, and copyrighted within the past 75 years may still be protected by copyright in the United States if a valid renewal registration was made during the 28th year of the first term of the copyright. If renewed, and if still valid under the other provisions of the law, the copyright will expire 75 years from the end of the year in which it was first secured.

Therefore, with one exception,* the United States copy-

---

*An Act of Congress, Private Law 92-60, effective December 15, 1971, provides that, subject to certain conditions, copyright is granted to the trustees under the will of Mary Baker Eddy, their successors, and assigns, in the work "Science and Health with a Key to the Scriptures" (entitled also in some editions "Science and Health" or "Science and Health; with a Key to the Scriptures"), by Mary Baker Eddy, including all editions thereof in English and translations heretofore published, or hereafter published by or on behalf of said trustees, their successors or assigns, for a term of seventy-five years from the effective date of this Act or from the date of first publication, whichever is later."

right in any work published or copyrighted more than 75 years ago (75 years from January 1st in the present year) has expired by operation of law, and the work has permanently fallen into the public domain in the United States. For example, on January 1, 1986, copyright in works first published or copyrighted before January 1, 1911, will have expired; on January 1, 1987, copyright in works first published or copyrighted before January 1, 1912, will have expired.

WORKS FIRST PUBLISHED OR COPYRIGHTED BETWEEN JANUARY 1, 1910, AND DECEMBER 31, 1949, BUT NOT RENEWED: If a work was first published or copyrighted between January 1, 1910, and December 31, 1949, it is important to determine whether the copyright was renewed during the last (28th) year of the first term of the copyright. This can be done by searching the Copyright Office records or catalogs, as explained above. If no renewal registration was made, copyright protection expired permanently on the 28th anniversary of the date it was first secured.

WORKS FIRST PUBLISHED OR COPYRIGHTED BETWEEN JANUARY 1, 1910 AND DECEMBER 31, 1949, AND REGISTERED FOR RENEWAL: When a valid renewal registration was made and copyright in the work was in its second term on December 31, 1977, the renewal copyright term was extended under the present act to 47 years. In these cases, copyright will last for a total of 75 years from the end of the year in which copyright was originally secured. Example: Copyright in a work first published in 1917, and renewed in 1945, will expire on December 31, 1992.

WORKS FIRST PUBLISHED OR COPYRIGHTED BETWEEN JANUARY 1, 1950, AND DECEMBER 31, 1977: If a work was in its first 28-year term of copyright protection on January 1, 1978; it must be renewed in a timely fashion to secure the maximum term of copyright protection provided by the present copyright law. If renewal registration is made during the 28th calendar year of its first term, copyright will endure for 75 years from the end of the year copyright was originally secured. If not renewed, the copyright expires at the end of its 28th calendar year.

UNPUBLISHED, UNREGISTERED WORKS: Before 1978, if a work had neither been "published" in the legal sense nor registered in the Copyright Office, it was subject to perpetual protection under the common law. On January 1, 1978, all works of this kind, subject to protection by copyright,

were automatically brought under the new Federal copyright statute. The duration of these new Federal copyrights will vary, but none of them will expire before December 31, 2002.

Derivative Works

In examining a copy (or a record or tape) for copyright information, it is important to determine whether that particular version of the work is an original edition of the work or a "new version." New versions include musical arrangements, adaptations, revised or newly edited editions, translations, dramatizations, abridgments, compilations, and works republished with new matter added. The law provides that derivative works are independently copyrightable and that the copyright in such a work does not affect or extend the protection, if any, in the underlying work. Under the 1909 law, courts have also held that the notice of copyright on a derivative work ordinarily need not include the dates or other information pertaining to the earlier works incorporated in it. This principle is specifically preserved in the present copyright law.

Thus, if the copy (or the record or tape) constitutes a derivative version of the work, these points should be kept in mind:

- The date in the copyright notice is not necessarily an indication of when copyright in all of the material in the work will expire. Some of the material may already be in the public domain, and some parts of the work may expire sooner than others.

- Even if some of the material in the derivative work is in the public domain and free for use, this does not mean that the "new" material added to it can be used without permission from the owner of copyright in the derivative work. It may be necessary to compare editions to determine what is free to use and what is not.

- Ownership of rights in the material included in a derivative work and in the preexisting work upon which it may be based may differ, and permission obtained from the owners of certain parts of the work may not authorize the use of other parts.

The Name in the Copyright Notice

Under the copyright statute in effect before 1978, the notice was required to include "the name of the copyright proprietor." The present act requires that the notice include "the

APPENDIX   E1:

RECORDATION   OF   TRANSFERS   AND CERTAIN   OTHER   DOCUMENTS

§ 201.3 [Reserved]

§ 201.4 Recordation of transfers and certain other documents.

(a) *General.* (1) This section prescribes conditions for the recordation of transfers of copyright ownership and other documents pertaining to a copyright under section 205 of Title 17 of the United States Code, as amended by Pub. L. 94-553. The filing or recordation of the following documents is not within the provisions of this section:

(i) Certain contracts entered into by cable systems located outside of the 48 contiguous States (17 U.S.C. 111(e); see 37 CFR 201.12);

(ii) Notices of identity and signal carriage complement, and statements of account, of cable systems (17 U.S.C. 111(d); see 37 CFR 201.11; 201.17);

(iii) Original, signed notices of intention to obtain compulsory license to make and distribute phonorecords of nondramatic musical works (17 U.S.C. 115(b); see 37 CFR 201.18);

(iv) License agreements, and terms and rates of royalty payments, voluntarily negotiated between one or more public broadcasting entities and certain owners of copyright (17 U.S.C 118; see 37 CFR 201.9);

(v) Notices of termination (17 U.S.C. 203, 304(c); see 37 CFR 201.10); and

(vi) Statements regarding the identity of authors of anonymous and pseudonymous works, and statements relating to the death of authors (17 U.S.C. 302).

(2) A "transfer of copyright ownership" has the meaning set forth in section 101 of Title 17 of the United States Code, as amended by Pub. L. 94-553. A document shall be considered to "pertain to a copyright" if it has a direct or indirect relationship to the existence, scope, duration, or identification of a copyright, or to the ownership, division, allocation, licensing, transfer, or exercise of rights under a copyright. That relationship may be past, present, future, or potential.

(3) For purposes of this section:

(i) A "sworn certification" is an affidavit under the official seal of any officer authorized to administer oaths within the United States, or if the original is located outside of the United States, under the official seal of any diplomatic or consular officer of the United States or of a person authorized to administer oaths whose authority is proved by the certificate of such an officer, or a statement in accordance with section 1746 of Title 28 of the United States Code; and

(ii) An "official certification" is a certification, by the appropriate Government official, that the original of the document is on file in a public office and that the reproduction is a true copy of the original.

(b) *Forms.* The Copyright Office does not provide forms for the use of persons recording documents.

(c) *Recordable documents.* Any transfer of copyright ownership (including any instrument of conveyance, or note or memorandum of the transfer), or any other document pertaining to a copyright, may be recorded in the Copyright Office if it is accompanied by the fee set forth in paragraph (d) of this section, and if the requirements of this paragraph with respect to signatures, completeness, and legibility are met.

(1) To be recordable, the document must bear the actual signature or signatures of the person or persons who executed it. Alternatively, the document may be recorded if it is a legible photocopy or other full-size facsimile reproduction of the signed document, accompanied by a sworn certification or an official certification that the reproduction is a true copy of the signed document. Any sworn certification accompanying a reproduction shall be signed by at least one of the persons who executed the document, or by an authorized representative of that person.

(2) To be recordable, the document must be complete by its own terms. (i) A document that contains a reference to any schedule, appendix, exhibit, addendum, or other material as being attached to the document or made a part of it shall be recordable only if the attachment is also submitted for recordation with the document or if the reference is deleted by the parties to the document. If a document has been submitted for recordation and has been returned by the Copyright

Office at the request of the sender for deletion of the reference to an attachment, the document will be recorded only if the deletion is signed or initialed by the persons who executed the document or by their authorized representatives. In exceptional cases a document containing a reference to an attachment will be recorded without the attached material and without deletion of the reference if the person seeking recordation submits a written request specifically asserting that: (A) The attachment is completely unavailable for recordation; and (B) the attachment is not essential to the identification of the subject matter of the document; and (C) it would be impossible or wholly impracticable to have the parties to the document sign or initial a deletion of the reference. In such exceptional cases, the Copyright Office records of the document will be annotated to show that recordation was made in response to a specific request under this paragraph.

(ii) If a document otherwise recordable under this indicates on its face that it is a self-contained part of a larger instrument (for example: if it is designated "Attachment A" or "Exhibit B"), the Copyright Office will raise the question of completeness, but will record the document if the person requesting recordation asserts that the document is sufficiently complete as it stands.

(iii) When the document submitted for recordation merely identifies or incorporates by reference another document, or certain terms of another document, the Copyright Office will raise no question of completeness, and will not require recordation of the other document.

(3) To be recordable, the document must be legible and capable of being reproduced in legible microform copies.

(d) *Fee.* For a document consisting of six pages or less covering no more than one title, the basic recording fee is $10. An additional charge of 50 cents is made for each page over six and each title over one. For these purposes:

(1) A fee is required for each separate transfer or other document, even if two or more documents appear on the same page;

(2) The term "title" generally denotes "appellation" or "denomination" rather than "registration," "work," or "copyright"; and

(3) In determining the number of pages in a document, each side of a leaf bearing textual matter is regarded as a "page."

(e) *Recordation.* The date of recordation is the date when a proper document under paragraph (c) of this section and a proper fee under paragraph (d) of this section are all received in the Copyright Office. After recordation the document is returned to the sender with a certificate of record.

(17 U.S.C. 205, 702, 708)

[43 FR 35044, Aug. 8, 1978]

APPENDIX   E2:

RECORDATION   OF   AGREEMENTS   BETWEEN
COPYRIGHT   OWNERS   AND   PUBLIC
BROADCASTING   ENTITIES

quest, the Copyright Office will issue an import statement permitting the importation of two thousand copies of the work to the name and address given under paragraph (b)(3)(vi) of this section.

(17 U.S.C. 601(b); 702)

[46 FR 12704, Feb. 18, 1981]

§ 201.9 Recordation of agreements between copyright owners and public broadcasting entities.

(a) License agreements voluntarily negotiated between one or more owners of copyright in published nondramatic musical works and published pictorial, graphic, and sculptural works, and one or more public broadcasting entities, and terms and rates of royalty payments agreed to among owners of copyright in nondramatic literary works and public broadcasting entities will be filed in the Copyright Office by recordation upon payment of the fee prescribed by this section. The document submitted for recordation shall meet the following requirements:

(1) It shall be an original instrument of agreement; or it shall be a legible photocopy or other full-size facsimile reproduction of an original, accompanied by a certification signed by at least one of the parties to the agreement, or an authorized representative of that party, that the reproduction is a true copy;

(2) It shall bear the signatures of all persons identified as parties to the agreement, or of their authorized agents or representatives;

(3) It shall be complete on its face, and shall include any schedules, appendixes, or other attachments referred to in the instrument as being part of it; and

(4) It shall be clearly identified, in its body or a covering transmittal letter, as being submitted for recordation under 17 U.S.C. 118.

(b) For a document consisting of six pages or less covering no more than one title, the basic recordation fee is $10; an additional charge of 50 cents is made for each page over six and each title over one.

(c) The date of recordation is the date when all of the elements required for recordation, including the pre-

scribed fee, have been received in the Copyright Office. A document is filed in the Copyright Office, and a filing in the Copyright Office takes place on the date of recordation. After recordation the document is returned to the sender with a certificate of record.

(17 U.S.C. 207 and 17 U.S.C. 118, 702, 708(11), as amended by Pub. L. 94-553)

[42 FR 16777, Mar. 30, 1977, as amended at 46 FR 33249, June 29, 1981]

§ 201.10 Notices of termination of transfers and licenses covering extended renewal term.

(a) *Form.* The Copyright Office does not provide printed forms for the use of persons serving notices of termination.

(b) *Contents.* (1) A notice of termination must include a clear identification of each of the following:

(i) The name of each grantee whose rights are being terminated, or the grantee's successor in title, and each address at which service of the notice is being made;

(ii) The title and the name of at least one author of, and the date copyright was originally secured in, each work to which the notice of termination applies; and, if possible and practicable, the original copyright registration number;

(iii) A brief statement reasonably identifying the grant to which the notice of termination applies;

(iv) The effective date of termination; and

(v) In the case of a termination of a grant executed by a person or persons other than the author, a listing of the surviving person or persons who executed the grant. In the case of a termination of a grant executed by one or more of the authors of the work where the termination is exercised by the successors of a deceased author, a listing of the names and relationships to that deceased author of all of the following, together with specific indication of the person or persons executing the notice who constitute more than one-half of that aurhor's termination interest: That author's surviving widow or widower; and all of that author's surviving children; and, where any of that author's children

SELECTED   BIBLIOGRAPHY:

BOOKS,   ARTICLES,
GOVERNMENT   DOCUMENTS,   ETC.

Aleinikoff, Eugene N. "Educational Implications of the New Copyright Law." In *Copyright and the Teaching/Learning Process*, pp. 4-10. Edited by Jerome K. Miller. Pullman, WA: Information Futures, 1977.

AECT [Association for Educational Communications and Technology]. *Copyright and Educational Media.* Washington, DC: AECT, 1977.

Association for Multi-Image. *Standard Pro-Forma Production and Staging Contracts.* Abington, PA [now Tampa, FL]: AMI, 1980.

Baumgarten, Paul A., and Farber, Donald C. *Producing, Financing and Distributing Film.* New York: Drama Book Specialists, 1973.

Becker, Gary H. *The Copyright Game.* Sanford, FL: Author, 1983.

Bentley, Martha A. *Copyright: Insights for the Christian Musician.* Chandron, NE: Jaybee Enterprises, 1980. (c/o 504 W. Second/Chadron, NE 69337)

Berk, Lee Eliot. "Legal Instruction for the College Music Student." *Performing Art Review* 3 (1972): 149-173.

Bierderman, Donald E; Gordon, Nicholas; and Ellner, Kenn. "Customary Contract Patterns and Problems in the Record Industry." In *Legal and Business Aspects of the Music Industry: Music, Videocassettes, and Records*, pp. 15-47. New York: Practising Law Institute, 1980.

Black's Law Dictionary. 5th ed. St. Paul: West Publishing Co., 1979.

Bloomer, Charles H. "Letters [to the Editor]: The Other Side." *Training* 22 (March 1985): 23.

Bomser, Alan; Bernstein, Mitchell; and Lewin, Jay. "Legal Problems Re: Music in Video Recordings of Motion Pictures." In *Legal and Business Aspects of the Music Industry: Music, Videocassettes, and Records*, pp. 629-692. New York: Practising Law Institute, 1980.

Boxer, Lester. "Dramatic Performing Rights in Dramatico-Musical Compositions: Scope of Protection." *Southern California Law Review* 34 (1961): 447-467.

Bronzo, John F. "Copyright—Infringement of Dramatico-Musical Rights—ASCAP License—*Robert Stigwood Group Ltd. v. Sperber.*" *Boston College Industrial and Commercial Law Review* 14 (1972- 1973): 1304-1321.

"Business Notes: A Thriller of a Deal." *Time* 126 (26 August 1985): 46.

Carroll, Lewis. *Alice's Adventures in Wonderland and Through the Looking-Glass.* New York: Collier Books, 1962.

Cavallo, Robert M., and Kahan, Stuart. *Photography: What's the Law?* 2nd ed. New York: Crown Publishers, 1979.

Chernoff, George, and Sarbin, Hershel. *Photography and the Law.* 5th ed. New York: Amphoto, 1977.

Coon, O. Wayne. "Some Problems with Musical Public-domain Materials Under United States Copyright Law as Illustrated Mainly by the Recent Folk-song Revival." In *ASCAP Copyright Law Symposium*, pp. 189-218. New York: Columbia University Press, 1971.

Copyright Clearance Center. Now You Can Photocopy and Still Comply with the Copyright Law. (brochure)

Corwin, Betty L. Director, Theatre on Film and Tape, The New York Public Library. Letter, 28 May 1985.

Crawford, Tad. *Legal Guide for the Visual Artist*. New York: Hawthorn Books, 1977.

Denham, Rena B. "The Problem of Musical Videodiscs: The Need for Performance Rights in Sound Recordings." *University of San Francisco Law Review* 16 (Fall 1981): 133-155.

Denicola, Robert C. "Copyright in Collections of Facts: A Theory for the Protection of Nonfiction Literary Works." In *Current Developments in Copyright Law 1982*, pp. 559-587. New York: Practising Law Institute, 1982.

Dern, Dixon Q. "Outline: Copyright—Subject Matter and Formalities; Motion Pictures and Other Audiovisual Works." In *Copyright: Selected Practical Approaches to Protection and Enforcement*, pp. 48-57. Edited by Paul D. Supnik, Margaret Saal, and David Carson. Beverly Hills: Los Angeles County Bar Association, 1984.

Does the Showing of Videocassette Tapes of Motion Pictures to Prison Inmates by Correctional Authorities Constitute an Infringement of Copyright? 65 Ops. Cal. Atty. Gen. 106 (1982).

Ducey, Maxine Fleckner. Wisconsin Center for Film and Theater Research, Madison, Wisconsin. Letter, 29 May 1985.

Edwards, David N. "Usages of Copyrighted Musical Works Permissible Without Acquiring a Copyright License, Assignment, or Release." *Journal of College and University Law* 6 (1979-1980): 363-384.

Ellingson, Carol A. "The Copyright Exception for Derivative Works and the Scope of Utilization." *Indiana Law Journal* 56 (1980-1981): 1-42.

Farber, Donald C. *Producing Theatre: A Comprehensive Legal and Business Guide.* New York; Drama Book Publishers, 1981.

Finkelstein, H. "ASCAP As an Example of the Clearing House System in Operation." *Bulletin of the Copyright Society of the U.S.A.* 14 (1966): 2-7.

Gary, Charles L. Letter. 12 June 1985.

Gaunt, Joseph H. "What to Cover in a Production Contract." *E & I TV* 15 (January 1983): 42-44.

Gertz, Ronald H.; Van Petten, Anita Ross; and Van Petten, Vance Scott. "Clearance of Rights." In *Producing for Motion Pictures and Television: A Practical Guide to Legal Issues,* pp. 3-92. Edited by Vance Scott Van Petten. Beverly Hills: Los Angeles County Bar Association, 1983.

Giblin, James Cross. "Tracking Down the Perfect Picture: Reflections of an Author of Informational Books." *CBC Features* 40 (1985-1986): unpaged.

Glick, Edwin, and Sutton, Michael. "Copyright Law for Producers of AV Programs." *AV Video* (March 1987): 60; 62-63.

Goldsborough, Robert. "*Murder in E. Minor*" (Book review). *Booklist* 82 (1 March 1986): 947.

Goldstein, Jack C. "Questions and Answers About the Performance of Music Under the New Copyright Law." In *Current*

Developments in Copyright Law, pp. 805-830. New York: Practising Law Institute, 1982.

Goldstein, Patrick. "Pop Eye: A Missing Person Is Found in the Nude." *Los Angeles Times*, 6 January 1985, Calendar p. 64.

Goldstein, Paul. "Derivative Rights and Derivative Works in Copyright." *Journal of the Copyright Society* 30 (February 1983): 209-252.

Goldway, Celia. "Copyright Infringement and the First Amendment." In *ASCAP Copyright Law Symposium*, pp. 1-30. New York: Columbia University Press, 1983.

Hampe, Barry. "Budgeting a Production Part I: Getting It Recorded." *Technical Photography* 18 (December 1986): 44-47.

Hampe, Barry. "Budgeting a Production Part II: Organizing It for an Audience." *Technical Photography* 19 (March 1987): 16; 21; 45.

Harris, Robert W. "Memorandum: Introductory Guide to Academic Risks of Copyright Infringement." *The Journal of College and University Law* 7 (1980-81): 328-345.

The Harry Fox Agency. Request for Non-Theatric Quotation. (mimeographed form, n.d.)

Hartnick, Alan J. "Performances at Schools and Colleges Under the 1976 Copyright Act." *Seton Hall Law Review* 8 (1977): 667-677.

Hearn, Edward R. "Legal Aspects of Video Production." *Video Systems* (August 1987): 44-60.

Helm, A. Brian, comp. *Nonprint Media and the Copyright Law: An Educator's Responsibilities and Rights*. N.p.: Anne Arundel County Public Schools, 1984.

Helm, A. Brian, comp. *Print Material and the Copyright Law: An Educator's Responsibilities and Rights.* N.p.: Anne Arundel County Public Schools, 1984.

Helm, Virginia. *Software Quality and Copyright.* Washington, DC: AECT, 1984.

History of the Litigation. F.E.L. Publications, Ltd., n.d.

Jaszi, Peter. "When Works Collide: Derivative Motion Pictures, Underlying Rights, and the Public Interest." *UCLA Law Review* 28 (April 1981): 715-815.

Kaplan, B. *An Unhurried View of Copyright.* New York: Columbia University Press, 1967.

Kaufman, Henry R. "Gnomon Copyright Case Revisited." *American Libraries* 11 (December 1980): 684-685.

Koenigsberg, I. Fred. ASCAP. Letter. 4 March 1985.

Komen, Edwin. Brylawski, Cleary & Leeds. Letter. 15 March 1985.

Korman, Bernard, "Music Performance Rights." In *Current Developments in Copyright Law 1979,* pp. 189-197. New York: Practising Law Institute, 1979.

Korman, Bernard. "Performance Rights in Music Under Sections 110 and 118 of the 1976 Copyright Act." In *Current Developments in Copyright Law 1979,* pp. 199-222. New York: Practising Law Institute, 1979.

Lane, Kathleen. "Libel and the Video Producer." *Videopro* 3 (July/August 1984); 24-25.

Lane, Kathleen. "The Model Release." *Videopro* 3 (November 1984): 66-67.

Langford, Michael J. "Copyright: Who Owns What?" *Industrial Photography* 35 (October 1986): 10, 12.

Lanham Act of 1946, 15 U.S.C. §§1051-1127.

Latman, Alan. "Annual Review of Copyright Cases: The Nuts and Bolts Are Finally Being Construed." *Journal of the Copyright Society of the U.S.A.* 29 (1982): 465-478.

Lawrence, J. S., and Timberg, B., eds. *Fair Use and Free Inquiry: Copyright Law and the New Media.* Norwood, NJ: Ablex, 1980.

Leavens, Thomas R. "Performing Arts & the Law." In *Law and the Arts—Art and the Law,* pp. 48-53. Chicago: Lawyers for the Creative Arts, 1979.

Lindey on Entertainment, Publishing and the Arts. 2nd ed. 3 vols. New York: Clark Boardman, 1984.

Los Angeles County Bar Association. Intellectual Property and Unfair Competition Section. *Producing for Motion Pictures and Television: A Practical Guide to Legal Issues.* Edited by Vance Scott Van Petten. Beverly Hills: Los Angeles County Bar Association, 1983.

"Lugosi's Privacy Rights Declared Dead." *Art & the Law* 5 (1980): 94-95.

Manning, Jack. "Leisure/Camera View: An Inside Look at Picture Agencies and Stock Houses." *New York Times*, 3 July 1977, pp. 25/27.

Marks, Henry. Harry Fox Agency. Phone conversation and letter, 12 July 1985.

Mathes, Charles. Director, the Rodgers and Hammerstein Theatre Library. Letter. 7 June 1985.

May, Carl W. Biological Photo Service, Moss Beach, CA. Letter. 29 May 1985.

Milbrodt, Bill. "Concerning Sound Tracks." *E & I TV* 17 (November 1985): 42-43; 54.

Miller, Jerome K. *The Copyright Directory: General Information* (vol. I). Friday Harbor, WA: Copyright Information Services, 1985.

Miller, Jerome K. "Copyright Protection for Bibliographic, Numeric, Factual, and Textual Databases." *Library Trends* 32 (Fall 1983): 199-209.

Miller, Jerome K. *Using Copyrighted Videocassettes in Classrooms and Libraries*. Friday Harbor, WA: Copyright Information Services, 1984.

Miller, Jerome K. *Video Copyright Guidelines for Pastors & Church Workers*. New York: National Council of the Churches of Christ, 1986.

Music Educators National Conference [et al.]. *The United States Copyright Law: A Guide for Music Educators*. N.p.: n.d.

National Federation of Local Cable Programmers. Letter to Access Producers. n.d.

Nevins, Francis M., Jr., "The Doctrine of Copyright Ambush: Limitations on the Free Use of Public Domain Derivative Works." *Saint Louis University Law Journal* 25 (1981): 58-86.

"New York Times' Unauthorized Use of Photograph on the Cover of Its Magazine Section Did Not Violate New York Civil Rights Law." *Entertainment Law Reporter* 4 (1 August 1982): 5-6.

Nimmer, Melville B. *Nimmer on Copyright: A Treatise on the Law of Literary, Musical and Artistic Property, and the Protection of Ideas*. 4 vols. New York: Matthew Bender, 1984, 1986.

Notice of Intention to Obtain a Compulsory License for Making and Distributing Phonorecords of Nondramatic Musical Works, 37 C.F.R. §201.18 (1986).

Notice of Objection to Certain Noncommercial Performances of Nondramatic Literary or Musical Works, 37 C.F.R. §201.13 (1986).

O'Malley, Brian S. "Fair Use and Audiovisual Criticism." *COMM/ENT* 4 (Spring 1982): 419-443.

Passman, Donald S., ed. *The Music and Recording Industry: Practical and Business Aspects.* Los Angeles: Entertainment Law Institute/University of Southern California Law Center, 1984.

Perrone, Vincent Louis. "Small and Grand Performing Rights? (Who Cared Before 'Jesus Christ Superstar')." *Bulletin of the Copyright Society of the U.S.A.* 20 (1972-72): 19-40.

"Personal Glimpses." *Reader's Digest* 127 (September 1985): 130.

"Presley Publicity Right Not Inheritable." *Art & the Law* 5 (1980): 95.

A Producer's Guide to Music Clearance. Los Angeles: Clearing House, Ltd., 1985.

"Questions and Answers on the ASCAP College and University License Agreement." In *Current Developments in Copyright Law 1979.* New York: Practising Law Institute, 1979.

Recordation of Agreements Between Copyright Owners and Public Broadcasting Entities, 37 C.F.R. §201.9 (1986).

Recordation of Transfers and Certain Other Documents, 37 C.F.R. §201.4 (1986).

Richardson, Alan, and Schwartz, Thomas. "What Media Managers Should Know About Copyrights." *E & I TV* 14 (October 1982): 74-78.

Rinzler, Carol E. "Whose Life Is It Anyway?" *Publishers Weekly* (19 April 1985): 20-22.

Rubin, E. Leonard. "Film and Video and the Law." In *Law & the Arts—Art & the Law,* pp. 65-81. Chicago: Lawyers for the Creative Arts, 1979.

Rudell, Michael I. *Behind the Scenes: Practical Entertainment Law.* New York: Law & Business/Harcourt Brace Jovanovich, 1984.

Samuel French, Inc. *1985 Basic Catalogue of Plays.* New York: Samuel French, n.d.

Sanchez, Ernest T. *Copyright and You—A Primer for Producers on Copyright and Fair Use.* Washington, DC: National Federation of Local Cable Programmers, n.d.

Sayers, Dorothy L. *Murder Must Advertise.* New York: Avon, 1933 (1967 printing).

Schools—State Music Festivals—Duplication of Copyrighted Works, 15 Ops. Kan. Atty. Gen. 202 (1981).

Seltzer, L. E. "Exemptions and Fair Use in Copyright: The 'Exclusive rights' Tensions in the New Copyright Act." *Bulletin of the Copyright Society of the U.S.A.* 24 (1977): 215-277; 279-337.

Seltzer, L. E. *Exemptions and Fair Use in Copyright, the Exclusive Rights Tensions in the 1976 Copyright Act.* Cambridge, MA: Harvard University Press, 1978.

Selz, Thomas, and Simensky, Melvin. *Entertainment Law: Legal Concepts and Business Practicies.* 3 vols. Colorado Springs, CO: Shepard's/McGraw-Hill, 1984.

Shapiro, Peter. "The Validity of Registered Trademarks for Titles and Characters After the Expiration of Copyright on the Underlying Work." In *ASCAP Copyright Law Symposium,* 69-103. New York: Columbia University Press, 1984.

Shemel, Sidney, and Krasilovksy, M. William. *More About This Business of Music.* New York: Billboard, 1974.

Shemel, Sideny, and Krasilovksy, M. William. *This Business of Music.* 5th ed. New York: Billboard Publication, 1985.

"Showing Video Cassettes to Prisoners Is 'Fair Use.' " *PTCJ* 29 (7 March 1985): 480-481.

Siegel, Richard J. "Non-Profit Musical Performance Societies and the 1976 Copyright Act: Selected Problems and Possible Solutions." *Northern Illinois University Law Review* 2 (Spring 1982): 449-470.

Singer, Laurence. *Contracts and Copyright: A Handbook for Visual Artists.* Washington, DC: Slide Registry of Artists, 1982.

Sinofsky, Esther R. *Off-Air Videotaping in Education: Copyright Issues, Decisions, Implications.* New York: R. R. Bowker, 1984.

Smith, Martha H. LIFE Picture Service. Letter. 29 May 1985.

Sobel, Lionel S. "A Practical Guide to Copyright Ownership and Transfer: The Differences Between Licenses, Assignments and Works Made for Hire." In *Copyright: Selected Practical Approaches to Protection and Enforcement,* pp. 41-47. Edited by Paul D. Supnik, Margaret Saal, and David Carson. Beverly Hills: Los Angeles County Bar Association, 1984.

Spataro, Stephen A. "Photography." In *Copyright: Selected Practical Approaches to Protection and Enforcement,* pp. 163-174. Edited by Paul D. Supnik, Margaret Saal, and David Carson. Beverly Hills: Los Angeles County Bar Association, 1984.

Sperber, Philip. *Intellectual Property Management: Law—Business—Strategy.* 3 vols. New York: Clark Boardman, 1983.

Spiegel, Irwin O. "Rights in Group Names." In *Legal and Business Aspects of the Music Industry: Music, Videocassettes, and Records,* pp. 207-214. New York: Practising Law Institute, 1980.

Stalos, Sam. "The Band in the Background." *AV Video* 6 (December 1984): 42-48.

Stalos, Sam. "Getting Away with It." *AV Video* 6 (December 1984): 8; 11.

Strong, William S. *The Copyright Book: A Practical Guide.* 2nd ed. Cambridge, MA: The MIT Press, 1984.

Sutak, Ken. *The Great Motion Picture Soundtrack Robbery: An Analyis of Copyright Protection.* Hamden, CN: Archon Book, 1976.

Talbot, William. Samuel French, Inc., New York. Letter. 29 May 1985.

Taubman, Joseph. *In Tune with the Music Business.* New York: Law-Arts Publishers, 1980.

Thomas J. Valentino, Inc. 1985 brochure.

Thompson, W. Robert. "Music Works, Sound Recordings and the New Copyright Law." In *Legal and Business Aspects of the Music Industry: Music, Videocassettes, and Records,* pp. 431-522. New York: Practising Law Institute, 1980.

"Training Today: Sources for Sounds." *Training* 21 (November 1984): 17.

"Training Today: What Rights Do You Buy." *Training* 22 (July 1985): 10; 12.

Tucker, William. "Using Image Libraries." *E & I TV* 17 (November 1985): 32-33; 36.

Tulchin, Hal. "Extras! Extras! Read All About 'Em!" *Videopro* 3 (November 1984): 22.

Turner, James L. "It's a Bird, It's a Plane Or Is It Public Domain?: Analysis of Copyright Protection Afforded Fictional Characters." *South Texas Law Journal* 22 (1982): 341-353.

United States Code Annotated. Title 17: Copyrights. St. Paul: West Publishing Co., 1977.

U.S. Congress. House. Committee of Conference. *General Revision of the Copyright Law, Title 17 of the United States Code.* H. Rept. No. 94-1733. 94th Cong., 2d sess., 1976.

U.S. Congress. House. Committee on the Judiciary. *Copyright Law Revision.* H. Rept. No. 94-1476. 94th Cong., 2d sess., 1976.

U.S. Congress. Senate. *An Act for the General Revision of the Copyright Law, Title 17 of the United States Code.* Pub. L. 94-553, 94th Cong., 1976, S.22.

U.S. Congress. Senate. Committee on the Judiciary. *Copyright Law Revision.* S. Rept. No. 94-473. 94th Cong., 1st sess., 1975.

U.S. Department of Commerce. National Bureau of Standards. Administrative Bulletin 78-28. 19 June 1978.

U.S. Department of Defense. Directive Number 5535.4 31 August 1984.

U.S. Library of Congress. Copyright Office. *Circular R1b: Limitations on the Information Furnished by the Copyright Office.* Washington, DC: Government Printing Office, 1979.

U.S. Library of Congress. Copyright Office. *Circular R2: Publications on Copyright.* Washington, DC: Government Printing Office, 1984.

U.S. Library of Congress. Copyright Office. *Circular R6: Obtaining Copies of Copyright Office Records and Deposits.* Washington, DC: Government Printing Office, 1985.

U.S. Library of Congress. Copyright Office. *Circular R7d: Mandatory Deposit of Copies or Phonorecords for the Library of Congress.* Washington, DC: Government Printing Office, 1982.

U.S. Library of Congress. Copyright Office. *Circular R15: Renewal of Copyright.* Washington, DC: Government Printing Office, 1979.

U.S. Library of Congress. Copyright Office. *Circular R15a: Duration of Copyright.* Washington, DC: Government Printing Office, 1984.

U.S. Library of Congress. Copyright Office. *Circular R21: Reproduction of Copyrighted Works by Educators and Librarians.* Washington, DC: Government Printing Office, 1978.

U.S. Library of Congress. Copyright Office. *Circular R22: How to Investigate the Copyright Status of a Work.* Washington, DC: Government Printing Office, 1985.

U.S. Library of Congress. Copyright Office. *Circular R31: Ideas, Methods, or Systems.* Washington, DC: Government Printing Office, 1984,

U.S. Library of Congress. Copyright Office. *Circular R32: Blank Forms and Other Works Not Protected by Copyright.* Washington, DC: Government Printing Office, 1984.

U.S. Library of Congress. Copyright Office. *Circular R34: Copyright Protection Not Available for Names, Titles, or Short Phrases.* Washington, DC: Government Printing Office, 1984.

U.S. Library of Congress. Copyright Office. *Circular R40b: Deposit Requirements for Registration of Claims to Copyright in Visual Arts Material.* Washington, DC: Government Printing Office, 1984.

U.S. Library of Congress. Copyright Office. *Circular R44: Cartoons and Comic Strips.* Washington, DC: Government Printing Office, 1983.

U.S. Library of Congress. Copyright Office. *Circular R45: Copyright Registration for Motion Pictures Including Video Recordings.* Washington, DC: Government Printing Office, 1980.

U.S. Library of Congress. Copyright Office. *Circular R56: Copyright for Sound Recordings.* Washington, DC: Government Printing Office, 1985.

U.S. Library of Congress. Copyright Office. *Circular R96 Section 201.20: Methods of Affixation and Positions of the Copyright Notice on Various Types of Works.* Washington, DC: Government Printing Office, 1985.

U.S. Library of Congress. Copyright Office. *General Guide to the Copyright Act of 1976.* Washington, DC: Government Printing Office, 1977/1978.

Wager, Willis. *A Musician's Guide to Copyright and Publishing.* Brighton, MA: Carousel Publishing, 1978.

Ward, Nicholas D. "Copyright in Museum Collections: An Overview of Some of the Problems." *The Journal of College and University Law* 7 (1980-81): 297-320.

Weil, Stephen E. "A Checklist of Legal Considerations for Museums." *The Journal of College and University Law* 7 (1980-81): 346-352.

Wigren, Harold E. "An Educator's Interpretation of the New Copyright Law, 1977." In *Copyright and the Teaching/Learning Process,* pp. 18-34. Edited by Jerome K. Miller. Pullman, MA: Information Futures, 1977.

Words and Phrases. St. Paul: West, n.d.

Zavin, Theodora. BMI. Letter. 12 March 1985.

Zavin, Theodore. "Music Performing Rights." In *Current Developments in Copyright Law,* pp. 781-785. New York: Practising Law Institute, 1982.

Zissu, Leonard. "Whither Character Rights: Some Observations." *Journal of the Copyright Society of the U.S.A.* 28 (1981): 121-138.

SELECTED BIBLIOGRAPHY:

COURT CASES

A. A. Hoehling v. Universal City Studios, Copyright L. Rep. (CCH) ¶25,096 (S.D.N.Y. 1979), *cert. denied*, U.S. Sup. Ct., Oct. 6, 1980, Docket No. 79-2029.

Alden-Rochelle, Inc. V. ASCAP, 80 F. Supp. 888 (S.D.N.Y. 1948).

Alfred Bell & Co. Ltd. v. Catalda Fine Arts, Inc., 90 U.S.P.Q. 153 (2d Cir. 1951).

Allied Artists Pictures Corp. v. Friedman, 68 Cal. App. 3d 127, 137 Cal. Rptr. 94 (1977).

"American Geophysical Union v. Texaco, Inc.," PTCJ 30 (9 May 1985): 32.

"[American Geophysical Union v. Texaco, Inc.] Photocopying Suit to Continue Despite Lack of Copying Specifics in Pleadings." *PTCJ* 32 (26 June 1986): 197-198.

April Productions, Inc. v. Strand Enterprises, Inc., 221 F.2d 292 (2d Cir. 1955).

Arrington v. The New York Times Company, 78 AD2d 839, *modified*, 55 NY2d 433, 449 N.Y.S.2d 941 (Ct. App. 1982).

Association of American Medical Colleges v. Mikaelian, 571 F. Supp. 144, 219 U.S.P.Q. 1032 (E.D. Pa. 1983), *aff'd*, 734 F.2d 3 (3d Cir. 1984).

217

Avedon v. Exstein, 141 F. Supp. 278 (S.D.N.Y. 1956).

Baker v. Selden, 101 U.S. 99 (1879).

Berlin v. E. C. Publications, Inc., 219 F. Supp. 911, 138 U.S.P.Q. 298 (S.D.N.Y. 1963), *aff'd*, 329 F.2d 541, 141 U.S.P.Q. 1 (2d Cir. 1964), *cert. denied*, 379 U.S. 822, 143 U.S.P.Q. 464 (1964).

Bleistein v. Donaldson Lithographing Co., 188 U.S. 239 (1903).

Booth v. Curtis Publishing, 1 Med. L. Rptr. 1784 (N.Y. App. Div. 1962).

Brandon v. The Regents of the University of California, 441 F. Supp. 1086 (D.Mass. 1977).

Broadcast Music, Inc. v. United States Shoe Corporation, 211 U.S.P.Q. 43, (C.D. Cal. 1980), *aff'd*, 217 U.S.P.Q. 224 (9th Cir. 1982).

Broadway Music Corporation v. F-R Publishing Corporation, 31 F. Supp. 817, 45 U.S.P.Q. 309 (S.D.N.Y. 1940).

Bruzzone v. Miller Brewing Co., 202 U.S.P.Q. 809 (N.D. Cal. 1979).

Buck v. Jewell-LaSalle, 283 U.S. 191, 9 U.S.P.Q. 17 (1931).

Burrow-Giles Lithographic Company v. Sarony, 111 U.S. 53 (1884).

Classic Film Museum, Inc. v. Warner Brothers, Inc., 453 F. Supp. 852, 199 U.S.P.Q. 265 (D.Me. 1978), *aff'd*, 597 F.2d 13, 202 U.S.P.Q. 467 (1st Cir. 1979).

College Entrance Book Company, Inc. v. Amsco Book Company, Inc., 33 F. Supp. 276, 45 U.S.P.Q. 516 (S.D.N.Y. 1940), *rev'd*, 119 F.2d 874, 49 U.S.P.Q. 517 (2d Cir. 1941).

Colten v. Jacques Marchais, 61 N.Y.S.2d 269 (N.Y. Mun. Ct. 1946).

Columbia Broadcasting System v. De Costa, 377 F.2d 315 (1st Cir. 1967), *cert. denied*, 389 U.S. 1007 (1968).

Columbia Pictures Industries, Inc. v. State of Wisconsin Department of Health and Social Services, Civil Action No. 83-C-1496-R (E.D.Wis. Jan. 21, 1985).

Corliss v. E. W. Walker Co., 64 F. 280 (C.C.Mass. 1894) (No. 3,152).

Cyril Russell v. Daniel A. Price, 448 F. Supp. 303 (C.D. Cal. 1977), *aff'd*, 612 F.2d 1123, Copyright L. Rep. (CCH) ¶25,125 (9th Cir. 1979), *cert. denied*, 446 U.S. 952, 100 S. Ct. 2919 (1980).

Dallas Cowboys Cheerleaders v. Scoreboard Posters, 600 F.2d 1184, 203 U.S.P.Q. 321 (5th Cir. 1979).

DC Comics, Inc. v. Filmation Associates, 486 F. Supp. 1273 (S.D.N.Y. 1980).

De Costa v. Columbia Broadcasting System, 520 F.2d 499 (1st Cir. 1975), *cert. denied*, 423 U.S. 1073 (1976).

Encore Music Publications v. London Film Productions, 89 U.S.P.Q. 501 (S.D.N.Y. 1951).

Excel Promotions Corporation v. Babylon Beacon, Inc., 207 U.S.P.Q. 616 (E.D.N.Y. 1979).

Factors Etc., Inc. v. Pro Arts, Inc., 579 F.2d 215 (2d Cir. 1978), *cert. denied*, 440 U.S. 908 (1979), *on remand*, 496 F. Supp. 1090 (S.D.N.Y. 1980), *rev'd*, 652 F.2d 278 (2d Cir. 1981), *cert. denied*, 456 U.S. 927 (1982), *on remand*, 541 F. Supp. 231 (S.D.N.Y. 1982), *reh'g denied*, 701 F.2d 11 (2d Cir. 1983), *vacated*, 562 F. Supp. 304 (S.D.N.Y. 1983).

Falk v. T. P. Howell & Co., 37 F. 202 (S.D.N.Y. 1888).

F.E.L. Publications, Ltd. v. Catholic Bishop of Chicago, 506 F. Supp. 1127, 210 U.S.P.Q. 403 (N.D. Ill. 1981), *rev'd*, 214 U.S.P.Q. 409 (7th Cir. 1982), *cert. denied*, 103 Sup. Ct. Rpt. 131 (1982), *aff'd in part, vacated in part*, 225 U.S.P.Q. 278 (7th Cir. 1985).

Filmvideo Releasing Corporation v. Hastings, 426 F. Supp. 690, 193 U.S.P.Q. 305 (S.D.N.Y. 1976).

Filmvideo Releasing Corporation v. Hastings, 509 F. Supp. 60, 212 U.S.P.Q. 195 (S.D.N.Y. 1981), *aff'd*, Copyright L. Rep. (CCH) ¶25,339 (2d Cir. 1981).

Fisher v. Dillingham, 298 F. 145 (S.D.N.Y. 1924).

Fisher v. Star Co., 231 N.Y. 414, 132 N.E. 133 (1921).

Foreign & Domestic Music Corp. v. Licht, 196 F.2d 627, 93 U.S.P.Q. 272 (2d Cir. 1952).

Galella v. Onassis, 487 F.2d 986, 1 Med. L. Rptr. 2425 (2d Cir. 1973).

Gershwin v. The Whole Thing Company, 208 U.S.P.Q. 557 (C.D. Cal. 1980).

Gilliam v. American Broadcasting Companies, 538 F.2d 14 (2d Cir. 1976).

Goldsmith v. Max, Copyright L. Rep. (CCH) ¶25,248 (S.D.N.Y. 1981).

Goodis v. United Artists Television, 425 F.2d 397 (2d Cir. 1970).

Green v. Luby, 177 F. 287 (S.D.N.Y. 1909).

Gross v. Seligman, 212 F. 930 (2d Cir. 1914).

Harper & Row v. Nation Enterprises, 557 F. Supp. 1067, 220 U.S.P.Q. 210 (S.D.N.Y. 1983), *rev'd*, 723 F.2d 195, 220 U.S.P.Q. 321 (2d Cir. 1983), *rev'd*, 225 U.S.P.Q. 1073 (1985).

The Harry Fox Agency v. Mills Music, Inc., 543 F. Supp. 844, 214 U.S.P.Q. 871 (S.D.N.Y. 1982), *rev'd*, 720 F.2d 733, 222 U.S.P.Q. 279 (2d Cir. 1983).

Henry Holt and Company v. Liggett and Myers Tobacco Company, 23 F. Supp. 302, 37 U.S.P.Q. 449 (E.D. Pa. 1938).

Iowa State University Research Foundation, Inc. v. American Broadcasting Companies, Inc., 463 F. Supp. 902, 203 U.S.P.Q. 484 (S.D.N.Y. 1978), *aff'd*, 621 F.2d 57, 207 U.S.P.Q. 97 (2d Cir. 1980).

Jerome v. Twentieth Century-Fox Film Corporation, 67 F. Supp. 736, 70 U.S.P.Q. 349 (S.D.N.Y. 1946), *aff'd per curiam*, 165 F.2d 785, 76 U.S.P.Q. 246 (2d Cir. 1948).

Jewelers' Circular Publishing Company v. Keystone Publishing Company, 274 F. 932 (S.D.N.Y. 1921).

Karll v. Curtis Publishing Company, 39 F. Supp. 836, 51 U.S.P.Q. 50 (E.D. Wis. 1941).

Lahiri v. Daily Mirror, 162 Misc. 776, 295 N.Y.S. 382 (1937).

Landsberg v. Scrabble Crossword Game Players, Inc., 212 U.S.P.Q. 155 (C.D. Cal. 1979), 212 U.S.P.Q. 159 (C.D. Cal. 1980), *vacated and remanded*, 736 F.2d 485, 221 U.S.P.Q. 1140 (9th Cir. 1984), *cert. denied*, 105 S. Ct. 513 (1984).

Landsberg v. Scrabble Crossword Game Players, Inc., 231 U.S.P.Q. 658 (9th Cir. 1986).

Le Mistral v. Columbia Broadcasting System, 3 Med. L. Rptr. 1913 (N.Y. App. Div. 1978).

Loew's Inc. v. Columbia Broadcasting System, Inc., 131 F. Supp. 165, 105 U.S.P.Q. 302 (S.D. Cal. 1955), *aff'd sub nom, Benny v. Loew's Inc.*, 239 F.2d 532, 112 U.S.P.Q. 11 (9th Cir. 1959), *aff'd per curiam* by an equally divided court, 356 U.S. 43, 116 U.S.P.Q. 479 (1958).

Lugosi v. Universal Pictures, 603 P.2d 425, 160 Cal. Rptr. 323 (Cal. 1979).

Lumiere v. Pathe-Exchange, 275 F. 428 (2d Cir. 1921).

Lumiere v. Robertson-Cole Distributing Corp., 280 F. 550 (2d Cir. 1922).

Macmillan Co. v. King, 223 F. 862, 18 Copy. Dec. 268 (D.Mass. 1914).

Marcus v. Rowley, 217 U.S.P.Q. 691 (9th Cir. 1983).

Meeropol v. Nizer, 417 F. Supp. 1201, 191 U.S.P.Q. 346 (S.D.N.Y. 1976), *aff'd in part, rev'd in part*, 560 F.2d 1061, 195 U.S.P.Q. 273 (2d Cir. 1977), *cert. denied*, 434 U.S. 1013, 196 U.S.P.Q. 592 (1978).

Miller Brewing Company v. Carling O'Keefe Breweries of Canada, 452 F. Supp. 429, 199 U.S.P.Q. 470 (W.D.N.Y. 1978).

Mills Music, Inc. v. State of Arizona, 187 U.S.P.Q. 22 (D.Ariz. 1975), *aff'd*, 201 U.S.P.Q. 437 (9th Cir. 1979).

N. Lindsay Norden v. Oliver Ditson Company, 13 F. Supp. 415, 28 U.S.P.Q. 183 (D.Mass. 1936).

Namath v. Sports Illustrated, 1 Med. L. Rptr. 1843 (N.Y. App. Div. 1975).

New York Times v. Sullivan, 1 Med. L. Rptr. 1527 (U.S. Supreme Court 1964).

Nichols v. Universal Pictures Corporation, 34 F.2d 145, 2 U.S.P.Q. 139 (S.D.N.Y. 1929), *aff'd*, 45 F.2d 119, 7 U.S.P.Q. 84 (2d Cir. 1930), *cert. denied*, 282 U.S. 902 (1931).

Orion Pictures v. Dell Publishing, 471 F. Supp. 392 (S.D.N.Y. 1979).

Pacific and Southern Company, Inc. v. Duncan, 220 U.S.P.Q. 859 (N.D. Ga. 1982).

Pacific and Southern Company v. Duncan, 572 F. Supp. 1186 (N.D. Ga. 1983), *aff'd in part, rev'd in part*, 744 F.2d 1490, 224 U.S.P.Q. 131 (11th Cir. 1984), *cert. denied*, 105 S.Ct. 1867 (1985), *remanded*, 618 F. Supp. 469, 228 U.S.P.Q. 141 (N.D. Ga. 1985), *aff'd*, 230 U.S.P.Q. 330 (11th Cir. 1986).

Pagano v. Charles Beseler Co., 234 F. 963 (S.D.N.Y. 1916).

Paulsen v. Personality Posters, Inc., 59 Misc.2d 444, 299 N.Y.S.2d 501 (1968).

Platinum Record Company v. Lucasfilm, Ltd., 566 F. Supp. 226 (D.N.J. 1983).

Prouty v. National Broadcasting Company, 26 F. Supp. 265 \D.Mass. 1939).

The Robert Stigwood Group v. Sperber, 457 F.2d 50 (2d Cir. 1972).

Rohauer v. Killiam Shows, Inc., 379 F. Supp. 723 (S.D.N.Y. 1975), *rev'd*, 551 F.2d 484 (2d Cir.), *cert. denied*, 431 U.S. 949 (1977).

Roy Export Company v. Columbia Broadcasting System, 503 F. Supp. 1137, 208 U.S.P.Q. 580 (S.D.N.Y. 1980), *aff'd*, 672 F.2d 1095, 215 U.S.P.Q. 289 (2d Cir. 1982), *cert. denied*, 459 U.S. 826 (1982).

Rubin v. Boston Magazine Co., 645 F.2d 80, 209 U.S.P.Q. 1073 (1st Cir. 1981).

Sailor Music v. The Gap Stores, Inc., 516 F. Supp. 923, 213 U.S.P.Q. 1089 (S.D.N.Y. 1981), *aff'd per curiam*, 688 F.2d 84 (2d Cir. 1981), *cert. denied*, 102 S.Ct. 2012 (1982).

Schnapper v. Foley, 471 F. Supp. 426, 202 U.S.P.Q. 699 (D.D.C. 1979), *aff'd*, 667 F.2d 102, 215 U.S. App. D.C. 59, *cert. denied*, 102 S.Ct. 1448, 455 U.S. 948, 71 L.Ed.2d 661.

Shapiro, Bernstein & Co., Inc. v. P. F. Collier & Son Co., 26 U.S.P.Q. 40, 20 Copy. Dec. 656 (S.D.N.Y. 1934).

Sony Corporation of America v. Universal City Studios, 480 F. Supp. 429, 203 U.S.P.Q. 656 (C.D. Cal. 1979), *rev'd in part, aff'd in part*, 659 F.2d 963, 211 U.S.P.Q. 761, 52 U.S.L.W. 4090 (U.S. Jan. 17, 1984), *reh'g denied*, 224 U.S.P.Q. 736 (1984).

Twentieth Century Music Corporation v. Aiken, 356 F. Supp. 271, 177 U.S.P.Q. 751 (W.D. Pa. 1973), *rev'd*, 500 F.2d 127, 182 U.S.P.Q. 388 (3d Cir. 1974), *aff'd*, 422 U.S. 151, 186 U.S.P.Q. 65 (1975).

Wainwright Securities Inc. v. Wall Street Transcript Corporation, 558 F.2d 91, 194 U.S.P.Q. 401 (2d Cir. 1977), *cert. denied*, 434 U.S. 1014, 196 U.S.P.Q. 864 (1978), *aff'g*, 418 F. Supp. 620, 194 U.S.P.Q. 328 (S.D.N.Y. 1978).

Walt Disney Productions v. Air Pirates, 345 F. Supp. 108, 174 U.S.P.Q. 463 (N.D. Cal. 1972), *modified*, 581 F.2d 751, 199 U.S.P.Q. 769 (9th Cir. 1978), *cert. denied*, 439 U.S. 1132 (1979).

Warner Brothers v. American Broadcasting Companies, 654 F.2d 205 (2d Cir. 1981).

Warner Bros. Pictures, Inc. v. Columbia Broadcasting System, Inc., 102 F. Supp. 141 (S.D. Cal.), *aff'd*, 216 F.2d 945 (9th Cir. 1954), *cert. denied*, 348 U.S. 971 (1955).

Welch v. Mr. Christmas, 8 Med. L. Rptr. 2366 (N.Y. Ct. Appl. 1982).

Wihtol v. Crow, 199 F. Supp. 682, 132 U.S.P.Q. 392 (S.D. Iowa 1961), *rev'd*, 309 F.2d 777, 135 U.S.P.Q. 385 (8th Cir. 1962).

Wihtol v. Wells, 231 F.2d 550, 109 U.S.P.W. 200 (7th Cir. 1956).

TABLE OF CASES

INDEX

NOTES:

NOTES:

Copyright Primer

ADDITIONAL PUBLICATIONS AVAILABLE
FROM COPYRIGHT INFORMATION SERVICES

Miller, J.K., Using Copyrighted Videocassettes in Classrooms, Libraries, and Training Centers.
2d. ed.   1988. $19.95

> Treats performance rights for videocassettes in schools, colleges, libraries, hospitals, churches, and industrial training centers.

Strong, W.S., The Copyright Book: A Practical Guide,
Second ed.   1984. $15.95.

> A copyright guide for authors, artists, photographers, etc.

Talab, R.S., Commonsense Copyright: A Guide to the New Technologies.   1985. $14.95.

> Applies the copyright law to all types of instructional hardware, from photocopiers to computer networks.

Vlcek, C.W., Copyright Policy Development: A Resource Book for Educators.   1987. $19.45.

> A handbook for writing school and college copyright policies. Includes sample policies which may be modified and adopted.

Official Fair-use Guidelines: Complete Texts of Four Official Documents Arranged for Use by Educators.
3d ed.   1987. $5.95.

> Includes the Congressional fair-use guidelines, plus the 1987 ICCA computer copyright guidelines.

Miller, J.K., Computer/Copyright Seminar, 1988.
[audio cassette and documents.]   1988. $24.88.

> Treats copyright issues facing educational computer users. The new ICCA copyright guidelines are included and discussed.

The Copyright Directory.   1985. $11.50.

>   Provides names, addresses, and phone numbers of thousands of individuals and organizations involved in the copyright law.

Miller, J.K., Church/Copyright Seminar, 1987.
[audio cassette and documents.]   1987. $24.87.

>   Treats video and music copyright issues facing church workers. Includes the new National Council of Churches video guidelines.

Miller, J.K., Video/Copyright Seminar, 1988.
[audio cassette and documents.]   1988. $24.88.

>   Treats videotaping off the air and off the satellite, using videocassettes in school and college settings, etc.

Order from:
COPYRIGHT INFORMATION SERVICES
Post Office Box 1460-A
Friday Harbor, WA 98250-1460